T H E
CHINESE
Microwave Cookbook
PEARLY HOH

Gulf Publishing Company
Houston, London, Paris, Zurich, Tokyo

The Author

Pearly Hoh has been demonstrating and lecturing to consumers and sales staff of a major distributor of microwave ovens in Malaysia for more than ten years. Previous to that, she worked as a fashion designer, in her spare time giving lessons in traditional Chinese cooking. She travels extensively on the job, seeking new ventures, discovering new techniques, particularly with reference to microwave cooking. On these trips, she exchanges notes on matters of home economics and the properties of ingredients. She has a gift of calming anxiety and overcoming reservations over microwave cooking, a quality that contributed to her success in this field.

Acknowledgments

The author thanks Tony Lau Tuck Mun for his encouragement and advice, and Jennifer Tan for helping with the organization and testing of recipes.

Dedication

to my late Dad, Jason Hoh Jueh Soh

Photographs: Yim Chee Peng, Culinary Studios
Food Stylist: Judy Chang
Graphics: Jeffrey Seow (preliminary pages)
Kelvin Sim (food chapters)
Calorie Count: Oy Heng Rasmussen
Crockery: Metrojaya, Yaohan, and Parkson Grand

This edition published in North America, 1995,
by Gulf Publishing Company
P.O. Box 2608
Houston, Texas 77525-2608

© 1989 Times Editions Pte Ltd
Times Centre, 1 New Industrial Road, Singapore 1953

Printed in Malaysia

ISBN 0-88415-275-8
Library of Congress Catalogue Card Number: 95-077129

CONTENTS

'Anyone preparing Chinese food should keep in mind that to the Chinese, food is not only pleasurable but a good deal more. It is a truism that food is life, but with the Chinese it is also health and a symbol of other good things such as luck and prosperity.

Heaven loves the man who eats well. At each meal a Chinese adds to his virtue, strengthening resistance to the ills of body and mind, curing ailments, or possibly, rendering himself capable of better work.'

INTRODUCTION

Asians are difficult to convince. Chinese are no different. Ten years of demonstrating microwave techniques to a mainly Chinese audience of consumers and sales staff has reinforced the truth of a personal maxim: 'Hearing is knowing, demonstrating is believing, but tasting – now that is convincing!'

Abandon the wok? Never! scoffed the doubting *tai-tais*. What about wok aroma? Closed door cooking chases away all the fragrance of food. Have you heard the latest radiation story. . .

So I took them through the process, deliberately choosing the most traditional Chinese recipes – stir-fried greens, Beggar Chicken, Drunken Chicken, Yuen Thai, and a host of Chinese New Year dishes, mother's home recipes, restaurant favorites. . . As the classes progressed, we even cooked Chung (rice dumplings) in the microwave oven.

Be cool. All the cooking is done in the microwave oven cavity. A microwave oven contains all the humidity, spray and heat. Nothing escapes into the kitchen. You are cool, your kitchen is clean.

Be organized. There is really no mystery. All it requires is a system in the preparation of ingredients. Each recipe in this book lists ingredients in groups. You are taken step by step through preparation and cooking.

Be adventurous. You'll be a great modern chef skilled in the art of traditional Chinese cooking. Put the microwave oven to full use. It's perfect for the braising of traditional recipes, sensational for double-boiled foods.

Be innovative. Pamper your taste buds, add or decrease herbs, or other ingredients as you become more familiar with recipes. Experiment with new flavors and ingredients. A comprehensive glossary and guide to buying and preparing ingredients is given in this book.

Stay traditional! Herbal soups are included. Cook these soups in you microwave oven for those who believe they can only be cooked the traditional way. No one will be the wiser.

Be healthier. Microwave cooking means less oil, flavors and essential vitamins and salts are sealed in, maintaining the richness of meats and the original color of vegetables. Seafood remains firm and intact.

Sek fun! Happy eating.

INGREDIENTS

Alkaline water   Sold in Chinese sundry shops or very cheaply in plastic bags, it is used to tenderize food. If too much is added, it leaves a stinging sensation on the tongue. A little alkaline water in the boiling water of lotus seeds helps you remove the clinging skin. If alkaline water is not available, use a little baking soda, which helps 'yellow' rice in Chung (rice dumpling) and gives it a crunchy texture, as well as preventing rice from sticking to bamboo leaves.

Arrowhead   A tuber that resembles an egg, about 4 cm (1¹/₂ in) long, smooth and beige. There are two varieties, one round and resembling water chestnuts and the other small and oval. Choose small ones, tear off loose brown leaves and peel the outer skin, then smash with the flat of a cleaver. Arrowroot is plentiful during Chinese New Year (January/February) when the Chinese are fond of slicing the round ones finely and deep-frying with salt like chips! The blandness of arrowroot makes it a good accompaniment for strong flavored meats.

Bamboo shoot   Use the canned variety, which is readily available. Fresh bamboo shoot requires extensive preparation prior to cooking.

Beans, salted black   Bottled, canned or in plastic bags, the most common or dry variety is preferred. These beans are loose whole soy beans preserved in salt and ginger. They are rather dry, and not messy to handle nor too salty. They also give a better aroma to cooked food than the moist variety that comes canned in some gravy.

Beansprouts   Beansprouts are slender white sprouts of beans. Snowy mounds on large flat woven rattan trays are present perennially in the wet markets of Asia. Two kinds may be observed: thick-short and thin-long. The thicker ones are neater, with a negligible 'tail'. Long ones appear straggly, having untidy brown 'tails', which should be plucked off. Beansprouts are mostly moisture and shrink considerably when fried dry, so are often only lightly cooked. Retain crisp freshness by soaking in water and storing in the refrigerator.

Bird's nest   Nests of swallows, lined with the hard thick or thin strands of gelatinous saliva. There are various grades, the most expensive being the rare blood-red bird's nest, believed to be made with the saliva of dying swallows, and more strength-imparting for that very fact. Soak for 3–4 hours till very soft and spongy, then pick out very fine feathers if any.

Bitter gourd   About 20 cm (8 in) long, tapering to a narrow end, the surface of the bitter gourd is warty and light to bright green. The more mature bitter gourds are the lighter green and less warty, the surface pattern being broader. The vegetable is sliced across, or at a diagonal, or halved lengthwise before slicing. To reduce bitterness, rub slices with salt, allow to stand for 30 minutes, then wash in boiling hot water.

Black moss seaweed   Loose and dry, the black moss seaweed resembles very fine black hair. This tasteless ingredient is cooked in specialty dishes on auspicious occasions, particularly Chinese New Year, for the Cantonese pronunciation of the product is *fatt choy*, which also means 'good luck'. It is often present in Chinese vegetarian dishes.

	CANTONESE	CHARACTERS
Alkaline water	kan suey	梘水
Almond	hung ngan	杏仁
flakes	hung ngan peen	杏仁片
Angled loofah	see kwa	丝瓜
Arrowhead	ngah koo	芽菇
Asparagus	loh shuen	芦笋
Bacon	for tooi	火腿
Chinese	lap yoke	腊肉
Bamboo shoot	chook shuen	竹笋
Barley	yee mai	玉米
Beans		
beansprouts	ngah choy	细豆芽菜
black	huck tau	黑豆
green	lok tau	绿豆
red	hoong tau	红豆
red bean paste	tau sar	豆沙
salted black	huck tau see	豆豉
Bird's nest	yeen wor	燕窝
Bitter gourd	foo kwa	苦瓜
Black moss seaweed	fatt choy	发菜
Borax	pang sar	硼砂
Broccoli	kai lan fah	芥兰花

Buddha's fruit This whole dried fruit resembles the kiwi fruit in size and color, but is slightly rounder, and the outer surface is a smooth, thin and fragile shell. It is believed to have a cooling effect on the body. In hot weather, simply crush the fruit and boil with winter melon and dried longans.

Cabbage All three kinds in these recipes are popular among Chinese as they keep well if dry when refrigerated. *Tientsin cabbage* tends to be more frequently used in cooking. There are two varieties of Tientsin cabbage. The smaller, oval, compact, white variety softens when cooked for a few minutes and is very sweet, while the commoner Tientsin cabbage is barrel-shaped, long and looser leafed, with more wrinkled yellow edges; it is crunchier when cooked. *Taiwanese cabbage* is, strictly speaking, not a cabbage, nor does it resemble one. It is a dark green leafy vegetable, about 15–20 cm (6–8 in) long, with the wide light green leaf stalks attached at the base. All cabbage varieties may be boiled, braised or cooked quickly with soy or oyster sauce.

Candied orange An orange with its top half slit two or more times, compressed to extract juice before being soaked in heavy syrup and dried. Available in Chinese medical halls and sundry shops.

Chiles Dried chiles are frequently used in Szechuan cooking, where they lend spicy hotness and flavor. Fresh chiles are sliced thinly and served with soy sauce as a dip by the Southeast Asian Chinese. When buying fresh chiles, choose the hotter slender pointed ones for cooking, and fat ones for garnishing. Similarly, when buying dried chiles, choose the pointed more wrinkled variety, which are more pungent and give a better flavor. The flatter, neater variety is dried by a chemical agent.

Chinese bacon These flat 1 cm ($^1/_2$ in) thick brownish strips of pork are marinated with soy sauce, wine and sugar, then dried in the autumn sun and stored for the winter. Cook in braised dishes for added flavor.

Chinese celery This is quite unlike English celery, which is broader and more crisp. Chinese celery grown in the highlands is broader, bigger and a paler green. As with all greens, choose crisp and fresh stalks. Chinese celery is highly aromatic, with a strong flavor. To reduce blood pressure, boil Chinese celery in water at medium heat till celery turns yellowish green. Drink on alternate days.

Chinese chestnuts These rich and delicious nuts are available all year though they are more abundant around July–August. First remove the loose outer shell, then soak the kernel overnight before removing its furry clinging skin. The way to do this is to use the point of a knife to separate the skin where it is attached in the folds of the nut. It is faster to parboil.

Chinese chives Chinese chives are long and narrow like spring onions but flat, darker green and sold without the bulb. They are more fibrous than spring onions or English chives. Except for flowering chives which are sweeter, they are seldom cooked on their own. Chives impart a welcome flavor and texture to certain foods, for example beansprouts, rice noodles, seafood and firm white beancurd squares.

Chinese parsley These are actually coriander leaves, strong flavored fan-shaped small leaves with a serrated edge, on fine stems about 15–20 cm (6–8 in) long, bunched together at the base. Usually chopped and thrown in for flavor and garnish after food is cooked.

	CANTONESE	CHARACTERS
Cabbage	pow choy	包菜
Taiwanese	siew pak choy	小白菜
Tientsin	wong ngah pak	绍菜(黄芽白)
Carrot	hoong lobak	红萝卜
Cashew nuts	yew tau	腰豆
Cauliflower	pow choy fah	包菜花
Celery	sai kuhn	茜芹
Chinese	kuhn choy	韮菜(九菜)
Chestnut		
Chinese	foong loot	栗子
water	mah tai	马蹄
Chilli	lat chiew	辣椒
dried	lat chiew kon	辣椒干
Chives	kow choy	
flowering	kow choy fah	
Chrysanthemum	chung hoe	茼蒿叶
leaves		
Cinnamon stick	yoke kwai pei	玉桂皮
Cloves	teng heong	丁香
Cucumber	cheng kwa	青瓜
yellow	loh wong kwa	老黄瓜
Cuttlefish	mak yee	墨鱼
dried	pat chow yee	八爪鱼
Dates	mut tzo	蜜枣
red	hoong tzo	红枣
Duck	ngap	鸭
waxed	lap ngap	腊鸭
Eggplant/Brinjal	ngai kwa	矮瓜

Soybean Varieties

1 Dried beancurd sheet
(*foo chook pei*)
2 Soft white beancurd
square
(*suey tau foo*)
3 Dried beancurd stick
(*foo chook*)
4 Firm yellow beancurd
(*tau yoon*)
5 Soybean curd
6 Dried sweet beancurd
sheet
(*tim chook*)

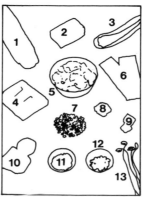

7 Soy beans
8 Fermented red beancurd
(*nam yee*)
9 Fermented white
beancurd
(*foo yee*)
10 Deep-fried beancurd ball/
square
(*tau foo pok*)
11 Preserved soybean paste
12 Salted black beans
13 Soybean sprouts

Chinese radish Salted and preserved Chinese radishes are frequently mentioned in this book: both are made from the same ingredient, the white Chinese radish. A fresh Chinese radish looks exactly like a carrot in size and shape, except it is white. Boiled with meat, it loses its pungency. Eaten raw, its tangy flavor makes it an excellent garnish. Make a *Chinese radish pickle:* shred, then squeeze in a cloth bag to remove moisture, before pickling in vinegar syrup. Refrigerate. Add pickled radish shreds when steaming fish or meat if you run out of ginger or simply wish to try a different flavor. *Salted radish* is whole Chinese radish (including the top leaves) sliced lengthwise, then coated heavily with salt. The slices are a dull dark brown, nearly 30 cm (12 in) long. They are not eaten, merely imparting flavor to soups and braised dishes. *Preserved Chinese radish,* on the other hand, are small pieces preserved in salt, sugar and a little soy sauce (sometimes also with a little chile and wine), then dried. The small golden brown chunks are sold in Chinese provision shops and emporiums and may be eaten raw or cooked to give a crisp texture to food. Teochews are fond of eating preserved radish raw with their *muay* or porridge.

Chinese sausage This dried, hard, narrow or thick cylindrical sausage is made of pork. It gives food a sweet fragrance: the Chinese love to steam a sausage or two on top of just cooked rice. Slice diagonally before eating.

Chinese water chestnuts Small 3–4 cm (1–2 in) crunchy and sweet white bulbs, covered with a dark brown skin which should first be peeled. Available canned, they may be eaten raw or cooked.

Chrysanthemum leaves Commonly called the 'steamboat vegetable' as it is a basic ingredient for Chinese steamboats, the slightly furry leaves are joined at the base. Cook very quickly. It is strong flavored but has a smooth, fine texture and is excellent roughage. It also rids one of the congested feeling caused by over-indulgence in meat.

Cloud ears See Fungi.

Cucumber, yellow This melon is far larger and heavier than any cucumber, being about 30–40 cm (more than a foot) long and broader. It is not eaten raw. Prepare by scrubbing clean and cut into pieces, retaining the tough skin which helps hold the white flesh together. Peel the skin and you will have mush instead of clear soup. The skin is discarded at the table.

Duck, waxed This delicacy is available during the Chinese New Year in Chinese emporiums and Chinatowns and is a convenient gift between family members during that period. Preserved in wine and salt, soaked in oil and dried, it is usually steamed or cooked with arrowroot, which absorbs the oil and saltiness of waxed duck.

Eggplant Also known as brinjal or aubergine. Chinese prefer the long purple variety to the green as the former is thinner skinned and the pulp has a finer texture. Choose smaller, young eggplants as they have fewer seeds. As the firm white flesh browns when cut and exposed to air, soak slices in water and drain just before cooking. This also prevents the slight bitterness that results with the discoloration.

Fish cake This deep-fried fish paste, often sliced or shredded before cooking with noodles or vegetable. Fish paste is fresh minced fishmeat molded into balls or round flat patties with flour, some saltwater, and borax which gives it a crunchy texture. If making fish paste at home, scrape flesh from skin and dry-blend till fine. Refrigerate in salt water.

	CANTONESE	CHARACTERS
Fish		
cake	yee peng	鱼饼
catfish	tong sut yee	泥鳅
pomfret	chong yee	鲳鱼
red snapper	hoong choe yee	红雀鱼
saltfish (soft)	moi heong	梅香
Spanish mackerel	sai toh	西刀鱼
threadfin	mah yow yee	马友鱼
Five-spice powder	ng heong fun	五香粉
Flour	meen fun	面粉
glutinous rice	lor mai fun	糯米粉
rice	chim mai fun	粘米粉
French beans	kwai tau	扁豆, 鬼豆 (乌龟豆)
Fungus		
cloud ear	wan yee	云耳
white	suet yee	雪耳
wood ear	mook yee	木耳
Galangal	lam keong	蓝姜
Garlic	shuen tau	蒜头
spring	kiew tau	乔头
Ginger	keong	姜
juice	keong chup	姜汁
pickle	suen keong	酸姜
young	chee keong	子姜
Gingko nut	pak kor	白果
Golden lilies	kum chum	金针
Green peas	chiang tau	青豆

Five-spice powder This is a powdered mixture of star anise, cloves, fennel, aniseed and cinnamon.

French beans These narrow bright green beans are about 12 cm (5 in) long, and flattened, though not to the extent of snow peas (mange-tout). Press lightly when choosing at the wet market; avoid old ones that feel hollow, as they are fibrous and have large seeds. Though softer in texture than snow peas, they are better flavored and sweeter. String first, that is, take a little off the top and tear off a string that runs down one edge, then pluck a little off the bottom and do the same for the other edge. French beans are usually sliced diagonally into 4 cm (1¹/₂ in) lengths before cooking.

Frogs *Teen kai* is the Cantonese name for paddy frogs, and this literally translates to 'paddy chicken'. The texture of the meat is smooth and fine, very like that of spring chicken. Bought live in wet markets or cleaned and frozen in supermarkets, all parts may be eaten but the head. A large frog may be cut into 6 pieces. Frog's legs bought on their own are costlier as they are the meatiest part.

Fungi All kinds add color and texture, and some also add a subtle flavor to other foods. They are often present in vegetarian dishes. Those sold dried must be soaked to soften before being shredded or cut into smaller pieces for cooking. Snip off the hard stem portions. *Cloud ear fungus* is flower-like, and smoother and finer in texture than wood ears and more translucent when soaked. *Wood ears* are 'two-faced', black on one surface and dark grey on the other. They are thick and shaped like ears and add a crunchy texture as they never soften with cooking. *White fungus* is not white but beige. Soaked, it expands to double or triple its size. Boil only lightly if you wish to retain its crispness. It is tasteless but cooked as a sweet or dessert. It has a cooling effect. See also Mushrooms.

Galangal This rhizome is bulkier and far harder than ginger, and there is sometimes a faint pinkish tinge. Simply scrub clean. A mere slice or two imparts a characteristic aroma to food. It is used more for braised meats, particularly duck. Substitute bay leaves.

Ginger This is also an underground rhizome, related to the galangal but with its own distinctive flavor. If ginger is mentioned in the recipe, use old ginger, which has a drier surface and is usually covered with a thin layer of sand. It is more fibrous and stronger-flavored. Young ginger, on the other hand, has a light and subtle flavor and is used for steamed dishes. Prepare both by scraping off the skin and slicing or shredding, as specified in the recipe.

Gingko nuts These mild-flavored nuts may be bought in their shells in supermarkets, Chinese medical halls or sundry shops. Both shell and nut are light beige. Prepare by shelling, then soak kernels in warm water before peeling the light brown-orange skin. A bitter embryo in the center must be removed. Either halve the nut to remove it or push it out with a sharp toothpick.

Golden lilies Dried buds of the lily, these are sometimes called golden needles. Snip off the hard knobs at either end and soak to soften before cooking. To emphasize the crunchy texture, knot two buds together.

Hairy marrow This resembles an above average sized cucumber, with a layer of fine white hair. It is eaten cooked, braised or in soups. Scrape off the furry skin and slice or shred the vegetable.

Herbs Precise measurements should be followed as flavors are strong. It is advisable to guess on the lighter side, at least until accustomed to the herb. A Chinese medical hall will supply any herbal mixture - all that is needed is a description of the main ingredient. Sundry shops and oriental emporiums also sell ready mixed packs for traditional stews (mutton and spare ribs, for example). These give clear instructions in English and Chinese.

Kale A dark green leafy vegetable with tough leaves and stout stems. The thick stem is the desired part of Chinese kale, though leaves are also eaten. The skin of the stem is tough, fibrous and indigestible while the pith is succulent. Kale attracts worms and farmers counteract the problem with heavy-handed use of pesticides. Rid the vegetable of pesticides before cooking: soak the whole plant, leaf down, in salt water for an hour or so. Peel off the tough skin of the main stem, then slice diagonally, exposing as much pith as possible.

Leeks The thicker the onion-like bulb and lower stem, the better. Leaves are light green, flat and broad. Tear off loose brown leaves and discard the top third of

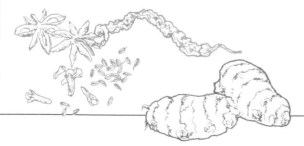

remaining leaves. The rest, the mainly white portion, is then sliced at a slant.

Long beans There are many varieties of these long cylindrical pods about 30 cm (12 in) long, with slight differences in intensity of green, from light to dark. Much depends on individual preference, but generally the lighter green variety is softer and common in many recipes. The darker green one, being thinner, harder and crunchier, is often cooked dry with preserved radish and minced pork. Long beans 'puff up' if kept longer than a few days and become fibrous and tasteless.

Longans The recipes refer to dried longans. Fresh ones are seasonal fruit, small and round with thin, light brown shells and a crunchy, succulent, translucent white flesh covering a hard, glossy black seed. Dried longans in their shell are sold in Chinese medical halls and sundry shops. More commonly available in the former are lumps of the dried longan meat. Wash the meat and pick out any shell residue.

Lotus root There are two varieties: a clean one that retains its crispness no matter how long it is cooked and a root that is sold caked in mud, which after cooking becomes reddish and soft, resembling potato in texture. The Chinese believe the crisp variety holds a cure for sore throats, and here it is: extract juice, mix with honey or rock sugar and simmer gently. Drink when cooled.

Lotus seeds These seeds have a brown skin that clings to the seed. The most convenient method of removal is to boil the seeds with alkaline water and, when cool, to rub off the skin. They can be cooked with spices (a favorite stuffing for roast duck) or sweet, along with other ingredients, such as dried longan.

Mooi choy There are two varieties, salty and sweet. This papery dark green and somewhat sticky leafy vegetable available at sundry shops has a strong sweetish smell. The leaves are joined at the base by light brown stalks, and the whole bunch is about 30 cm (12 in) long. It is shredded and steamed with pork or chicken, and is commonly found simmering with strips of belly pork darkened with soy sauce next to a pot of white Teochew rice porridge. Chinese ladies in confinement after childbirth are given *mooi choy* for roughage as fresh greens are believed to cause 'wind'.

Mushrooms Use fresh ones where these are available, in exactly the same way as dried mushrooms. Do not soak in water as you would the dried ingredient - simply clean under running water. The most common for the recipes here is the *black mushroom*, called Shiitake by some. It has a distinctive flavor and darkens clear soups, and is available for far ranging prices, depending on quality. Choose plump ones with undamaged white under-surfaces. If using dried black mushrooms, cut off the entire hard stem. *Button* and *straw* mushrooms are chosen more for shape and texture than flavor, while abalone mushrooms are sweet.

Mustard cabbage This tender leafy vegetable is about 30 cm (12 in) long, and all parts may be eaten with a minimum of preparation as the stems are tender and without a tough skin. Stems are narrow and grooved. Flowers are small, bright yellow and edible. Simply wash and cut to lengths required in the recipe.

	CANTONESE	CHARACTERS
Hairy marrow	moh kwa/ chit kwa	节瓜
Herbs, Chinese		
Buddha's fruit	loh hon kor	罗汉果
ginseng	pow sum/ tong sum	当参
kei chee	kei chee	杞子
kum cho	kum cho	甘草
magnolia petals	pak hup	白合
pak kei	pak kei	北芪
tong kwai	tong kwai	当归
wai sun	wai sun	汇山
yoke chok	yoke chok	肉竹
Honey	mut tong	蜜糖
Kale	kai lan choy	芥兰
Leek	shuen	大蒜
Lettuce	sang choy	生菜
Long beans	tau kok	长豆/豆角
Longan	longan	龙眼
Lotus		
leaf	leen yip	莲叶
root	leen ngou	莲藕
seed	leen chee	莲子

Flavourers

1 Screwpine leaf
2 Galangal
3 Young ginger
4 Chilli
5 Szechuan pepper
6 Sour plums
7 Tamarind
8 Pickled ginger

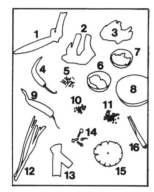

9 Dried chilli
10 Black peppercorns
11 White peppercorns
12 Spring onion
13 Candied winter melon
14 Cloves
15 Candied orange
16 Cinnamon stick

Dried Ingredients

1 Chinese bacon
2 Fish cake
3 Wood ear fungus
4 Cloud ear fungus
5 Black moss seaweed
6 Green beans
7 Chinese sausage
8 Red beans
9 Dried cuttlefish

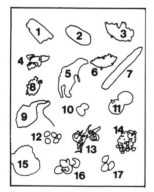

10 Red dates
11 Water chestnuts
12 Lotus seeds
13 Dried golden lilies
14 Black beans
15 White fungus
16 Dried prawns
17 Gingko nuts

Chinese Ingredients from the Medical Hall

1   *Pak kei*
2   Buddha's fruit
3   Dried longan
4   Rock sugar
5   *Wai sun*
6   *Tong kwai* (sliced)
7   *Tong kwai*
8   White fungus
9   Dried magnolia petals
    (*pak hup*)

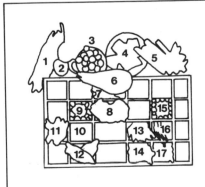

10   *Kei chee*
11   *Yoke chok*
12   Bird's nest
13   Ginseng
     (*tong sum*)
14   Dried tangerine peel
15   Lotus seeds
16   Ginseng
     (*pow sum*)
17   Red dates

	CANTONESE	CHARACTERS
Mooi choy, sweet	mooi choy	梅菜
Mushroom		
abalone	pow yee koo	鲍鱼菇
button	moh koo	磨菇
dried black	toong koo	冬菇
straw	cho koo	草菇
Mustard cabbage/ green	kai choy	芥菜
salted	hum choy	咸菜
Noodles		
cellophane	fun see	冬粉 (粉丝)
deep-fried	yee meen	依面
rice	mai fun (meehoon)	米粉
rice sheets	hor fun	夥条 (河粉)
thick yellow	meen	粗面
wantan	wantan meen	云吞面
Onion		洋葱
spring onion	tai choong tau	
Orange		
candied	khut peng	柑饼
Oyster	hoe	蚝
dried	hoe see	干蚝
sauce	hoe yau	蚝油

Noodles The most commonly used noodles are the *yellow noodles* made of wheat flour and alkaline water. There are several kinds, varying in shape (cylindrical or flat) and thickness of strands, and fresh, dried or deep-fried. *Wonton noodles* are dried thin strands of egg noodles. Fresh and dried noodles need no washing, but pour boiling water through deep-fried noodles to remove any rancid oil. *Cellophane noodles* are dried thin white strands of green bean flour. Soak in water to soften, then add to boiling stock at the last cooking step, as the they almost cook instantly. Overcooking causes starchiness. *Rice noodles* come in sheets or strands. Sheet rice noodles are fresh and should be cooked on the same day or refrigerated for a few days only. They may be sold already cut into wide flat strips. Choose the finer textured sheets as these look better. Strands of *rice vermicelli* are dry, brittle, translucent when dry and white when cooked. Soak in cold water till soft before cooking. Do not soak in hot water or the strands lose their elasticity and break easily when fried.

Oyster, dried These give a distinct sweet flavor when boiled in soups.

Persimmon The dried fruit, dark brown, flattened and coated with rice flour, is sold in oriental emporiums and Chinese medical halls. Wash and slice finely.

Persimmon slices add sweetness and are an ingredient in cooking sweet brews.

Sauces *Barbecue sauce* is glossy blackish brown, very thick, almost paste-like, but can be poured with a little difficulty. Its texture resembles tomato paste. It is made of soybean paste, papaya, wheat flour, sugar and salt, and is added in cooking or is present at the table, as a condiment for roast chicken and pork. *Hoisin sauce* is black and also like tomato paste in texture. It is made of soy beans, wheat flour, salt, sugar, vinegar, garlic, chile and sesame oil. An excellent dip for salads, there is also a red variety. *Hot bean sauce* is reddish brown and its ingredients are not too finely blended. It is made of whole kidney beans, coarsely chopped or whole salted soy beans, chiles, onions, garlic and vinegar. It is often called *tau pan cheong*. Hot bean sauce is a common base in Szechuan cooking. It is sold in glass or plastic jars. *Plum sauce* is a thick sweet-sour sauce made of Chinese plums. It is a popular dip for meats, particularly duck, and is also a common ingredient in meat marinades. *Soy sauce* is made of fermented soy beans, wheat or barley flour, salt, sugar and yeast. It brings out the flavor of foods and no Chinese kitchen is without it. There are dark and light brown varieties and countless 'grades'; use dark soy sauce as a browning agent when roasting meats in the microwave oven.

Sharksfin Buy loose and moist or prewashed and dried sharksfin in the supermarket or oriental emporiums. Soak dried sharksfin in water and parboil with ginger and wine, then remove particles of skin before cooking.

Shrimp Dried shrimp must be soaked to soften before being chopped or pounded. As they are slightly salty, taste before adding salt. Dried shrimp paste is dried shrimp blended to a paste and salted before being dried into purplish brown cakes. Use either the dried product or the thick saucy paste sold in jars.

Snow peas Also known as mange-tout, they are exactly like pods of shell peas, only much flatter as they have very much smaller seeds. When buying, choose the darker green young ones with very small seeds. String them as you would French beans, but leave whole. See French beans.

Soybean products Protein-rich soybean products are used in Chinese cooking much more frequently than soy beans, which are difficult to digest. *Deep-fried beancurd balls and squares* are porous fried beancurd. They do not break as easily as fresh beancurd squares (firm or soft), and may be stuffed more easily. They may also

	CANTONESE	CHARACTERS
Padi frog	teen kai	田鸡
Parsley	yim sai	蕃芫茜
Pepper		
black	huck vu chiew	黑胡椒粉
Szechuan	far chiew	花椒
white	pak vu chiew	白胡椒粉
Peppers/Capsicum		
green	chiang lat chiew	青辣椒
red	hoong lat chiew	红辣椒
Persimmon	kai sum chee	鸡心翅
Pineapple	wong lai	菠萝（黄梨）
Pig's spleen	chee wang lei	猪横舌
Pork, Chinese barbecued	char siew	叉烧
Prawns	har	虾
freshwater	tarm suey har	淡水虾
tiger	chou har	草虾
Pumpkin	kum kwa	南瓜（金瓜）
Quail's egg	ngum chuen tan	鹌鹑蛋
Radish		
Chinese	lobak	萝卜
preserved Chinese	choy poh	菜蒲
salted Chinese	tai tau choy	大头菜
Rice		
cooked	fahn	饭
glutinous	lor mai	糯米
long grain	mai	米

	CANTONESE	CHARACTERS
Sauce		
barbecue	tim cheong	甜酱
hoisin, black	hoisin	海鲜酱（黑）
hoisin, red	hoisin	海鲜酱（红）
hot bean	tau pan cheong	豆板酱
oyster sauce	hoe yow	蚝油
plum	suen mooi cheong	酸梅酱
soy sauce, dark	huck yow	黑酱油
soy sauce, light	see yow	酱油（生抽）
Sausage, Chinese	lap cheong	腊肠
Scallop	kong yee chee	干贝（江鱼翅）
Screwpine leaves	cheenloi yip	香叶
Sesame		
oil	ma yow	麻酒
seeds	chee ma	芝麻
Shallot	choong tau chai	小葱头
Sharksfin	yee chee	鱼翅
Shrimp	har chai	小虾
dried	har mai	干虾米
paste, dried	ma lai chan	马拉盏
Snow peas/ mange-tout	hor lan tau	荷兰豆
Sour plum	suen mooi	酸梅
Soy bean	wong tau	黄豆
deep-fried beancurd balls/ squares	tau foo pok	豆腐包
deep-fried soft beancurd squares	chow suey tau foo	炸水豆腐
dried beancurd sheets	foo chook pei	腐皮
dried beancurd sticks	foo chook	腐竹
dried sweet beancurd sheets	tim chook	甜竹
fermented red beancurd	nam yee	南乳
fermented white beancurd	foo yee	腐乳
firm white beancurd squares	tau foo	白豆腐
firm yellow beancurd squares	tau yoon	黄豆干
preserved soy beans	meen see	豆酱
soft white beancurd squares	suey tau foo	水豆腐
soybean sprouts	tai tau ngah	大豆芽菜
Spinach	por choy	菠菜
Star anise	pak kok	八角
Szechuan vegetable	char choy	榨菜

be braised or sliced thin for salads. *Deep-fried soft beancurd* is dark golden brown outside and soft fine beancurd inside. *Dried beancurd sheets* are thin, large, dried, cream-colored sheets sold folded in sundry shops. Wipe clean with a damp cloth before using. *Dried beancurd sticks* are cream-colored thin, brittle sticks of dried beancurd that require soaking in water to soften before use. *Dried sweet beancurd sheets* are 12 cm (5 in) long, rectangular, hard, flat, dark golden sheets. Wipe with a damp cloth, then deep-fry in oil before cooking to prevent from breaking. *Fermented beancurd* is fresh beancurd fermented with salt and rice wine. It is pungent and may be red (fermented with hoisin and chiles) or white. The most commonly used processed beancurd is *firm* or *soft beancurd squares*. Both are made from soybean juice, lime and water, the quantity of water determining the soft/firm texture. *Firm yellow beancurd squares* may be rectangular, not square, and are similar to the firm white ones, except for the presence of five-spice powder.

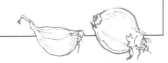

Vegetables

1 Hairy marrow
2 Yam bean
3 Salted radish
4 Old cucumber
5 Angled loofah
6 Bitter gourd
7 Tientsin cabbage
8 Preserved Chinese radish
9 Kale

10 Chinese radish
11 Water convolvulus
12 Taiwan cabbage
13 Mustard cabbage
14 Szechuan vegetable
15 Celery (English)
16 Chinese celery
17 Young corn
18 Chrysanthemum leaf

Spring garlic This is strong flavored and crunchy. Use all parts from the bulb to top leaves, discarding only loose brown leaves and the clump of roots at the base. The leaves are fibrous.

Szechuan pepper Dark brown and wrinkled, this has a finer aroma though it is not as hot as black or white pepper. It is commonly used in Szechuan cooking, hence its name.

Szechuan vegetable This small cabbage-like plant is a product of Shanghai, preserved in salt and chile powder in earthen jars. It is brownish green and coated with moist red chili powder, but may be sold clean of the powder. Wash (soak for a while if you prefer a less salty vegetable), then shred into matchstick strips or slice thinly. It retains its crunch even when boiled for a long time.

Tamarind pieces Whole tamarind is sliced very thinly and dried. The pieces are round, wavy at the edge, and being a cross-section of the tamarind, the following would be visible: a dark rim of skin, translucent light pulp, and perhaps a smaller hard center representing a seed. It gives a sour flavor to food and is added to steaming fish. Unlike tamarind pulp, it leaves no dark residue.

Water convolvulus A leafy vegetable with long, narrow, hollow stems and leaves shaped like arrowheads. There are two varieties - a finer textured one grown on land and a coarse convolvulus that grows wild along ponds.

Watercress Chinese watercress has very long stems, about 60 cm (24 in) from root to shoot. Leaves appear along about half of the stem and short white root-hairs at nodes along the rest of the stem. The root portions may be used to make stock as they add sweetness and flavor. Use only the tender young leaves and stems as a vegetable.

White fungus See Fungi.

Wine Unless otherwise indicated, use rice wine where wine is mentioned.

Winter melon Larger than the dessert watermelon, this has a less porous white meat and dark green skin. Scrape off the skin and remove coarse pulpy seeds before cooking. Candied winter melon is the white meat cut into 1 cm ($^1/_2$ in) thick sticks, coated in heavy syrup and dried so that the sugar crystalizes on the sticks. Sold in plastic packs in sundry shops and oriental emporiums, they are favored by children who eat them raw. Chinese use them to sweeten herbal brews.

Wonton **skins** Sold in supermarkets, these are creamy, moist, fresh, 6–7 cm ($2^1/_2$–3 in) square wrappers made of wheat flour, egg and alkaline water, used to wrap minced pork for *dim sum* foods. The meat sticks to the wrapper. *Wonton* skins are sold in stacks, lightly coated with flour to prevent sticking.

Wood ears See Fungi.

Yam This oval tuber covered with a rough, dark brown skin causes itchiness when handled. Remove the itch by rubbing with salt. There exists a variety that remains hard even after prolonged cooking. Soft-textured yams ooze a white sap when the cut exposed end is scraped with a fingernail. If the cut end shows fine dark purple dots and lines, the yam will be soft after cooking.

	CANTONESE	CHARACTERS
Tamarind, dried pieces	assam pei	亞三皮
Vinegar	cho	醋
black	hak cho	黑醋
Water convolvulus	oong choy	甕菜
Watercress	sai yeong choy	西洋菜
Wine		
glutinous rice	lor mai chow	糯米酒
rice	mai chow	米酒
Winter melon	toong kwa	冬瓜
candied	toong kwa tong	冬瓜茼
Yam	woo tau	芋头
Yam bean	sah kot	芜菁 (沙葛)

Yam bean The skin is light brown and the flesh is crunchy and sweet, making yam bean a popular choice for salads. Peel and shred for cooking, and add wedges of yam bean to sweeten soups. Substitute jicama.

THE MICROWAVE CHEF

Microwave Basics

Microwaves They may be likened to light and sound waves. They are not related at all to the more powerful x-rays or ultra-violet rays. Those who say they are a form of radiation are absolutely right, because 'radiation' is a general term, meaning to disperse from a source in waves or rays through the air, that is, without using wires.

Magnetron In the microwave oven, the source of microwaves is the magnetron. When the oven is switched on and the power button activated, the magnetron becomes active and emits waves.

Properties Microwaves have the properties of reflection, transmission and absorption. Microwaves are *reflected* by metal, hence they cannot reach anything placed inside a metal container. Similarly, they cannot escape from the cavity of the oven which is metallic (even the glass door has a wiremesh layer). Microwaves are *transmitted*, that is, they pass through other materials such as glass, ceramic, plastic and paper. Microwaves are *absorbed* by any substance that contains water, fat or sugar.

Cooking Microwaves penetrate any food substance to a depth of 3–4 cm (1–2 in). They cause the food particles to vibrate at super-speed, and this energy is converted into heat. The cooking is completed by conduction, that is to say the heat is transferred from hotter areas to cooler areas, cooking the rest of the food.

Cooking with Microwaves

Moist, no fat This is the key to successful microwave cooking. Choose recipes that are cooked by moisture - steaming, boiling, braising, blanching. Foods that require fat and oil for a change of flavor are not as successful. Deep-frying is impossible and there is real risk of fire if you try to heat oil for deep-frying in the microwave oven; an incredibly high heat is absorbed by oil.

Browning food Foods do not brown readily in the microwave oven. You may find the following tips on browning useful.
1 Fat absorbs heat and if you remove foil covering fatty portions of a meat, these will crisp and brown lightly.
2 Baste with oil to give a better crisp to roasts. Oil increases the temperature of the meat surface.

3 A browning dish, preheated, will brown food beautifully if you press food down, turning so that all surfaces make contact with the base of the dish.

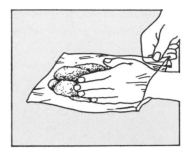

4   Soy sauce, the ubiquitous flavorer of Chinese recipes, is an excellent browning agent. In fact, soy sauce is also a far better agent for bringing out food flavors than salt, which dehydrates and toughens meat.

Wok aroma What deters many people from conversion to the microwave oven is the misconception that 'wok aroma' is lost in enclosed cooking. In traditionally stir-fried dishes, sauces are sprinkled round the side of the hot wok at the last stage of cooking, to release a fragrance. In the microwave oven, we put in the sauce first, giving time for heat to be absorbed and hence release the aroma.

Small, not large You gain a definite time advantage when you cook small quantities of food in the microwave oven. Large amounts are more quickly cooked the conventional way. The microwave oven is best therefore for family meals and when entertaining small groups.

4   Raise large portions of roast on a rack for more even distribution of heat. When meat is heated, fat melts to the bottom, and this area will absorb more heat.

Arrange foods Whether cooking, defrosting or freezing, food should be arranged to take advantage of the principles of microwave cooking. Remember the following:

1   Microwave activity is greater at edges, less at the center. Pieces of food should be placed at the edge of any container. If they are of unequal size, thicker portions should be placed at the edge or corners of square containers where they will cook more quickly than the thinner portions in the center. Cook large quantities of food evenly by stopping the cooking cycle halfway and stirring so that food at the edges changes places with food in the center.

Cover Covering the food will prevent drying of some dishes, speed cooking and prevent spattering. The most common cover is cling or plastic wrap. Since pressure is built up within a completely enclosed container, however, it is necessary to cover loosely or to leave a gap through which steam may escape. Alternatively, cover with paper or a plastic plate. Warning: Remember to uncover cling wrap away from yourself, so that steam escapes in the opposite direction.

2   Food cooks quicker in hot spots, so place the container or larger portions of meat in this place. (See 'Hot and cold spots' in the section on 'Your Microwave Oven' below.)

3   Single layers of food cook evenly. A large lump cooks at the edge first. So freeze foods in single layers and do not overlap food if you can help it.

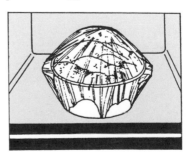

Shielding food These parts must be shielded with foil (dull surface out) to prevent overcooking and drying out: thinner pieces, parts sensitive to increased microwave activity such as fatty meat and sharp corners like projecting bone. Ensure that foil does not touch the sides of the oven.

Food skins Food that has skin or membrane, such as liver, tomato and fish, if they are to be left whole, should be pierced or slit, to leave a steam vent.

Cooking Times

Output and time Two main factors that decide the cooking time of the same quantity of food are the energy output (expressed in watts) and the internal capacity of the oven (expressed in cubic feet). Recipes in this book give the cooking times of an oven with energy output of 650W, and a capacity of 1.4 cubic feet. It takes 1 minute 50 seconds exactly to boil a 225 ml (8 fl. oz) Pyrex cup of water. Decrease time by 15 seconds per minute for a 700W oven and increase it by 20 seconds per minute for a 500W oven.

Starting temperature This affects cooking time. Recipes in this book give ingredients at room temperature. Defrost foods taken from the freezer and allow more time for foods just removed from the refrigerator.

Increasing quantity of food When you change quantities in the recipes, remember that the times do not necessarily change in direct proportion. It is always better to under-cook as you can always finish cooking. You cannot reverse the process if you over-cook food! Of course, 'doneness' is a matter of personal taste, and you will discover with practise how to master the art to your desire.

Standing time As a great deal of heat is generated within the food, you can prevent overcooking by removing the food container from the microwave oven at a specified time, and covering the container with foil (dull surface out). Standing times are given for individual recipes and should be followed.

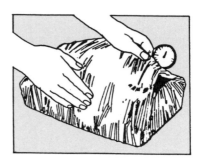

Your Microwave Oven

Metal box The microwave oven is simply a metal box which contains an electronic device, the magnetron. When the power is switched on, the magnetron generates microwaves and these are directed into the oven cavity. Within the cavity, they are absorbed by food particles but reflected off metal. Never operate an oven without food in the cavity as you may damage the magnetron.

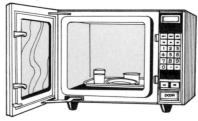

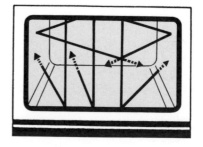

Hot and cold spots No matter what the claims of the manufacturer, the distribution of microwaves is not even. Test you oven for hot and cold spots by placing numbered slices of processed cheese all over the cooking base. The ones that heat first will become wavy first. Note the hot spots and place food here to cook faster.

Buying a microwave oven Check the adequacy of the following features.
1 *Door:* there should be a wiremesh screen in the glass door and a choke seal, which is a safety device surrounding the oven window on the inside of the door, a safety barrier between the window and the edge of the door.
2 *Vents:* they allow the steam to escape from the oven cavity and there should be instructions on cleaning vents at regular intervals.
3 *Cavity:* the smoother the internal surface, the easier to clean; the cavity should light up when the oven is operating.
4 *Controls:* these are the Start/cook, Power, Stop and a Timer which indicates minutes and seconds. The naming of power controls vary, some ovens adopting numbers, others percentages and still others indicators such as High, Defrost, etc. A table may be found in the section on Equivalents.

Optional extras These are the turntable, an aid to even cooking; a temperature probe that can be programmed to stop the power when food reaches a particular temperature; auto-sensors that sense when food is cooked by monitoring humidity of the oven cavity.

Study the manual It is most important you read all cautionary notes and the manufacturer's instructions. As with all electronic products, particularly care must be observed in the use, cleaning and servicing of your microwave oven, and the manual will list all these.

Accidents Should the oven fall or receive knocks, send it for a thorough check, even if it is not dented.

Servicing the oven Keep a note in your kitchen giving date of purchase, the distributing agent's address and telephone number, and important dates of servicing and repair. If possible, make a contract with your agent to service annually.

Equivalents

POWER

Microwave Power Levels	Percentage
High	100%
Medium-High	80%
Medium	60%
Medium-Low	40%
Low	20%

WEIGHTS AND MEASURES

You are strongly urged to purchase a set of spoon and cup measures, as spoon and cup measures are given in most recipes.

For all other measurements, both metric and imperial measures are stated. The following equivalents for liquids may be of some help.

Imperial	Cup/Spoon	Metric
	1 teaspoon	5 ml
	1 tablespoon	20 ml
1 fl oz	1½ tablespoons	30 ml
2 fl oz	¼ cup	60 ml
4 fl oz	½ cup	110 ml
5 fl oz	⅔ cup	150 ml
6 fl oz	¾ cup	175 ml
8 fl oz	1 cup	225 ml
16 fl oz	2 cups	450 ml
20 fl oz	2½ cups	560 ml
35 fl oz	4 cups	1 liter

(3 teaspoons equal 1 tablespoon)

MICROWAVE-SAFE EQUIPMENT

Microwaves are reflected by metal, so they cannot go through metal to cook food inside metallic utensils. Metallic parts cause arcing, noisy sparks that may damage the magnetron. Microwaves go through most other materials: glass, ceramic, stoneware, claypots, bamboo and wood, paper.

Ovensafe test Test your container unless the manufacturer states it is microwave-safe. Leave the container next to a Pyrex glass of water in the oven for two minutes, with the power set at high. The water should be hot and your utensil cool. Do not try to test any utensils without food or water as it may damage the magnetron.

Heat resistance Is the container heat resistant? Though the container is not heated itself, heat will be transferred from hot food to the container by conduction. Ovensafe glass and ceramics are microwave-safe.

Common errors Examine your container carefully. Some of the common mistakes are:
- ceramic plates with a metal rim or designer's signature
- crystal which looks like glass but contains lead
- cartons made of waxed material or polyfoam, both of which melt – into the hot food
- staples or glue in paper containers

Brand names A list follows. Check it for suitability of containers such as Melamine and Corningware in the microwave oven.

Round versus square Round containers are better than containers with corners. Microwave activity concentrates at the corners, cooking food placed there much faster. This can work to your advantage if you cook food of uneven shape. Chicken drumsticks, for example, should be placed with the larger end at the corners.

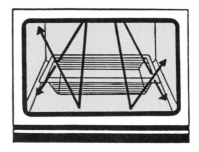

Browning dish A utensil you will need is a browning dish. This is a heavy ceramic-glass container with a thin layer of metal oxide in the base which is heated by microwaves. The browning dish is heated for a few minutes in the oven and the food is then pressed down in it, usually with a little oil, to brown its surfaces. The browning dish is the only container you may heat in the microwave oven without food in it.

Paper Paper plates and absorbent paper are useful 'containers'. Roast nuts, sesame seeds and anchovies and reheat foods on paper plates. Foods with fat that

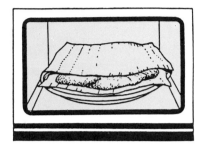

melts when heated crisps better if placed on several layers of absorbent paper.

Roasting duck For the same reason, you may need a roasting rack. This lifts the food off the moisture that collects at the bottom of a container. The space below roasting food also helps distribute microwaves evenly all round.

Is it Safe?

Aluminium foil	Use dull surface out, covering only according to manufacturer's instructions. Covering a third of the food surface is generally safe.	Oven roasting rack	Yes, if manufacturer claims it is microwave ovensafe.
		Metal roasting rack	No
Brown paper bags	No, as they are waxed and will burn.	Oven roasting bags	Yes
Browning dish	Yes. Be sure to handle with oven gloves.	Paper towels and napkins	Yes, excellent for drying herbs, and for crisping nuts and other foods. Also useful for heating high-fat convenience food like Chinese sausages. Paper dehydrates and ignites, so do not re-use it. Do not use paper which has nylon or other synthetics in it as these may also ignite.
Claypots and pottery mugs	Asian earthenware is safe. Some glazes, however, may contain metal and these are not safe. Check with ovensafe test.		
Corelle	Yes, except for those with glued-on handles.	Plastic	
		Melamine	Yes, for less fatty food, and for short periods.
Corningware	Only those without a metallic rim.	'Ovensafe'	Yes. Check if manufacturer claims it is heat resistant.
Dinnerware		Tupperware	Use the new range which is marked microwave-safe.
'Microwave-safe'	Yes		
Not marked	Oven-test first		
Metal-rimmed	No	Plastic wrap/cling wrap	Yes, but not in contact with food. Some kinds 'leak' into the food.
Gold/silver designer signature	No		
Glassware/ceramic		Waxed paper	Not in contact with food, particularly fatty foods which reach high temperatures. It may be used as a tent to cover containers and prevent spattering.
'Ovensafe'	Yes		
Not marked	No, as it may not be heat resistant.		
Grill pan	No		
Metal containers	No	Wooden stirrers, spoons and skewers	For short cooking periods only. Do not leave in the oven cavity if there are metal parts.
Metal twist-ties	No		

Black Chicken Herbal Soup (p. 27)

SOUPS

I n the microwave oven, soup is beautifully clear and flavors of food strong. These are advantages in Chinese cooking, which emphasizes flavor, shape and texture of ingredients.

Recipes in this section include those that are traditionally double-boiled to achieve a particularly clear soup. Coconut Soup, for example, requires 4 hours of double-boiling time, so that only advance orders of this soup are accepted by restaurants. It cooks in only 1 hour in the microwave oven.

Soup may be reheated in any container, such as a heatproof glass/ plastic jug, cups or soup bowls. Do not fill more than two-thirds full or soup may boil over. It is always covered - with a casserole lid, plastic plate or plastic wrap (with either a gap for a steam vent or plenty of room for steam build-up).

We have included here a recipe for Black Chicken Herbal Soup. Imbibed regularly, this brings reward in strength of body and mind, and (some believe) sexual vigor.

Bak Kut Teh

Serves 10
Cooking time: 60 mins
Preparation: 10 mins
K cal: 200/serve

Ingredients
1 kg (2 lb 3 oz) spare ribs
150 g (5 oz) sugar-cane
10 g (⅓ oz) *kei chee*
8 g (¼ oz) *tong kwai*
10 g (⅓ oz) *pak kei*
2 star anise
10 cloves
1 slice *kum cho*
6 cups hot water

A
1 tablespoon light soy sauce
½ teaspoon salt

Preparation

Cut spare ribs into bite-size pieces.

Remove hard skin of sugar-cane and cut into 5 cm (2 in) lengths, the thickness of a thumb. Smash sugar-cane strips with the flat side of a kitchen chopper.

Cooking

Combine all ingredients except ingredients A, in a 5 liter (5 qt) casserole. Cover and microwave on power MEDIUM-LOW for 1 hour.

Immediately after the cooking cycle, add ingredients A and let casserole STAND for 20 minutes before serving.

NOTE: *This brings back memories of midnight suppers with the fragrance of herbs wafting through the air.*

Black Bean Beef Soup

Serves10
Cooking time: 1 hr 9½ mins
Standing time: 20 mins
Preparation: 15 mins
K cal: 80/serve

Ingredients
100 g (3½ oz) black beans
250 g (8½ oz) beef

A
½ teaspoon Szechuan
    pepper
½ tablespoon oil
20 g (¾ oz) ginger, sliced
2 star anise

6 cups water
1 teaspoon salt

Preparation

Soak black beans. Remove skin and wash in a strainer.

Cut beef into 2 cm (¼ in) cubes.

Cooking

Combine ingredients A in a 5 liter (5 qt) casserole. Microwave on power HIGH for 1½ minutes, uncovered.

Add remaining ingredients, cover and microwave on power HIGH for 8 minutes. Then simmer on power MEDIUM-LOW for 1 hour.

Let casserole STAND for 20 minutes before serving.

Black Chicken Herbal Soup

(photo page 24)

Serves 4
Cooking time: 45 mins
Standing time: 10 mins
Preparation: 10 mins
K cal: 120/serve

Ingredients

1 black chicken, 500 g (1 lb
   1 oz)
20 g (¾ oz) *tong kwai*
6 cups hot water

A
3 tablespoons rice wine
1 teaspoon salt

Preparation

Wash and clean the chicken. Wash *tong kwai* lightly.

Cooking

Combine chicken, *tong kwai* and hot water in a 3 liter (3 qt) casserole and microwave on power MEDIUM-LOW for 45 minutes, covered.

Immediately after the cooking cycle, add ingredients A, cover and let casserole STAND for 10 minutes before serving.

Catfish Black Bean Soup

Serves 10
Cooking time: 53 mins
Preparation: 10 mins
K cal: 65/serve

Ingredients

300 g (10 oz) catfish

A
100 g (3½ oz) black beans
30 g (1 oz) ginger
1 tablespoon oil

5 cups hot water
1 teaspoon salt

Preparation

Clean and gut catfish. Cut into 3 cm (1 in) pieces.

Wash and soak black beans in clean water overnight. Scrape skin off ginger and slice thinly.

Cooking

Combine ingredients A in a 5 liter (5 qt) casserole. Microwave on power HIGH for 3 minutes, uncovered.

Add remaining ingredients, cover and microwave on power LOW for 50 minutes.

NOTE: *This soup is believed to cure a recurrent bleeding nose when imbibed regularly.*

Coconut Soup

(photo page 29)

Serves 4
Cooking time: 1 hour
Preparation: 20 mins
K cal: 535/serve

Ingredients
1 coconut

A
4 dried black mushrooms
100 g (3½ oz) lean pork
50 g (2 oz) ham
6 red dates
1²/₃ cups water

hand towels
1½ cups hot water

Preparation

Saw off a section 3 cm (1 in) from the top of the coconut for the cover. Discard water in the coconut and wash.

Soak dried black mushrooms to soften. Dice mushrooms and lean pork. Cut ham into strips.

Wash red dates and discard stone.

Combine prepared ingredients A in the coconut. Cover with the top section of the coconut.

In a 5 liter (5 qt) casserole, shape hand towels to form a ring for the coconut to sit on.

Cooking

Place coconut on the hand towel ring and pour 1½ cups hot water into the casserole. Cover with the top section of coconut and micro-wave on power LOW for 1 hour.

Mixed Herbal Chicken Soup

Serves 4
Cooking time: 1 hr
Standing time: 20 mins
Preparation: 10 mins
K cal: 80/serve

Ingredients
300 g (10 oz) chicken breast
15 g (½ oz) *pak kei*
10 g (⅓ oz) *kei chee*
10 g (⅓ oz) ginseng (*tong sum*)
5 g (⅕ oz) *tong kwai*
6 cups hot water
1 teaspoon salt

Preparation

Wash chicken and remove skin and fat. Wash all Chinese herbs lightly.

Cooking

Combine all ingredients except salt in 5 liter (5 qt) casserole. Cover and microwave on power MEDIUM-LOW for 1 hour.

Immediately after the cooking cycle, stir in salt and let casserole STAND for 20 minutes, covered, before serving.

NOTE: *If you are intimidated by the thought of buying Chinese herbs, the proprietor of a Chinese medicinal hall will be able to help you by picking the right mixture. Mention the ingredients, or simply state the kind and quantity of meat you wish to cook. Variations are slight. If you are not accustomed to herbal brews, proceed cautiously, adding a little at a time and tasting while cooking.*

Coconut Soup (p. 28), Beancurd with Egg Sauce (p. 110), Stuffed Green Peppers (p. 144)

Old Cucumber Oyster Soup

Serves 10
Cooking time: 1 hr 20 mins
Standing time: 20 mins
Preparation: 10 mins
K cal: 70/serve

Ingredients
300 g (10 oz) old cucumber
30 g (1 oz) dried oysters
30 g (1 oz) red dates
300 g (10 oz) spare ribs
6 cups hot water
1½ teaspoons salt

Preparation

Scrape skin off old cucumber and cut into bite-sized pieces.

Wash dried oysters. Wash red dates and discard the stone. Wash and cut spare ribs into bite-sized pieces.

Cooking

Combine all ingredients except salt in a 5 liter (5 qt) casserole. Cover and microwave on power MEDIUM-LOW for 1 hour and 20 mins.

Immediately after the cooking cycle, stir in salt. Let casserole STAND for 20 minutes before serving.

NOTE: *Another Chinese soup believed to stabilize body temperature.*

Peanuts and Pigtails

Serves 10
Cooking time: 55 mins
Preparation: 10 mins
K cal: 300/serve

Ingredients
700 g (1 lb 9 oz) pig's tail
150 g (5 oz) pre-cooked
    peanuts
80 g (3 oz) salted radish
8 red dates
6 cups water
1½ tablespoons light soy
    sauce

Preparation

Clean and cut pig's tail into bite-sized pieces.

Wash salted radish to remove excess salt and slice thinly. Wash red dates and discard the stone.

Cooking

Combine all ingredients except light soy sauce in a 5 liter (5 qt) casserole.

Microwave on power HIGH for 10 minutes, uncovered. Then cover and simmer on power MEDIUM-LOW for 45 minutes.

Immediately after the cooking cycle, stir in light soy sauce and serve.

Salted Vegetable Duck Soup

Serves 10
Cooking time: 1 hr 20 mins
Standing time: 20 mins
Preparation: 15 mins
K cal: 30/serve

Ingredients
500 g (1 lb 1 oz) duck
    pieces
200 g (7 oz) salted mustard
    cabbage
60 g (2 oz) tomatoes
20 g (¾ oz) ginger
1 teaspoon sugar
6 cups hot water
1 teaspoon salt

Preparation

Discard skin and fat of duck pieces.

Wash salted mustard cabbage to remove excess salt, then cut into bite-sized pieces.

Cut tomato into wedges. Scrape skin off ginger and slice thinly.

Cooking

Combine all ingredients in a 5 liter (5 qt) casserole. Cover and microwave on power MEDIUM-LOW for 1 hour and 20 minutes.

Let the casserole STAND for 20 minutes before serving.

Sharksfin Soup

Serves 6
Cooking time: 8 mins
Standing time: 5 mins
Preparation: 15 mins
K cal: 150/serve

Ingredients
A
150 g (5 oz) sharksfin
100 g (3½ oz) crabmeat
100 g (3½ oz) cooked
    chicken, shredded
1 teaspoon ginger juice
4 cups hot chicken stock

B
30 g (1 oz) water chestnut
    powder
1 teaspoon wine
2 teaspoons salt
¼ cup water

1 egg, beaten

Cooking

Combine ingredients A in a 3 liter (3 qt) casserole. Cover and microwave on power HIGH for 6 minutes.

Add combined ingredients B and microwave on power HIGH for 2 minutes, uncovered.

Immediately after the cooking cycle, stir in beaten egg. Cover and let casserole STAND for 5 minutes before serving.

Snow Drop Soup

Serves 10
Cooking time: 21 mins
Standing time: 10 mins
Preparation: 15 mins
K cal: 35/serve

Ingredients
10 g (⅓ oz) white fungus
100 g (3½ oz) green peas

A
50 g (2 oz) carrot
50 g (2 oz) onion
4 dried black mushrooms,
    soaked
150 g (5 oz) chicken breast
5 cups chicken stock
1½ teaspoons salt

Preparation

Soak white fungus to soften, then discard water. Dice carrot, onion, softened black mushrooms and chicken.

Cooking

Combine ingredients A in a 4 liter (4 qt) casserole. Microwave on power HIGH for 6 minutes, uncovered. Then cover and simmer on power MEDIUM for 15 minutes.

Add the remaining ingredients, cover the casserole and let it STAND for 10 minutes before serving.

Szechuan Hot Soup

Serves 6
Cooking time: 10 mins
Preparation: 20 mins
K cal: 60/serve

Ingredients
A
1½ teaspoons cornstarch
2 tablespoons water
80 g (3 oz) soft white
    beancurd square (*suey
    tau foo*)
1 teaspoon salt
3 tablespoons black vinegar
1 teaspoon sugar

B
50 g (2 oz) Szechuan
    vegetable
100 g (3½ oz) chicken meat
80 g (3 oz) bamboo shoot
4 dried black mushrooms
5 g (⅕ oz) wood ear fungus
    (*mook yee*)
3 cups chicken stock

Preparation

Mix cornstarch with 2 tablespoons water. Combine ingredients A in a 3 liter (3 qt) casserole.

Shred Szechuan vegetable, chicken and bamboo shoot. Soak mushrooms and wood ears to soften before shredding.

Cooking

Cover casserole containing ingredients B and microwave on power HIGH for 8 minutes.

Add ingredients A and microwave on power HIGH for 2 minutes, uncovered.

Winter Melon Soup

Serves 10
Cooking time: 1 hr
Preparation: 20 mins
K cal: 70/serve

Ingredients
1 winter melon, 2 kg (4 lb 6
    oz)
100 g (3½ oz) lean pork
5 red dates
3 dried black mushrooms
10 g (⅓ oz) dried scallops
6 dried oysters
2 cups hot water

Preparation

Wash winter melon and cut off a section 2 cm (1 in) from the top for the cover. Scoop out the seeds and pulp to leave behind a 1½ cm (½ in) thick shell.

Dice lean pork. Wash red dates and discard the stone. Soak dried black mushrooms to soften before slicing thinly.

Wash dried scallops and break into smaller pieces. Wash dried oysters.

Mix the prepared ingredients with 2 cups hot water and pour into the winter melon shell. Replace the cover and secure with toothpicks.

Cooking

Place prepared melon in a 5 liter (5 qt) casserole. Cover with cling wrap and microwave on power LOW for 1 hour.

Fish Egg Roll (p. 37), Spinach with Prawn Sauce (p. 142)

FISH

This low-calorie food is believed by the Chinese to be good for the eyes and brain, but definitely to be avoided when suffering from a cold. Fish cooked in the microwave oven retains its shape, moisture and flavor so well it requires only a little garnish. It can, moreover, be cooked in its serving plate.

As flavors are truly represented, however, fish must be fresh before cooking. When buying fish, check that eyes are clear and bright, gills are red and moist, the body firm, and it has no unpleasant fishy smell.

If cooking fish whole, prepare by
- removing the eyes, which are covered with membrane and may burst,
- scoring the sides to split the skin,
- covering the thinner portions, such as the tail end and fins, with aluminium foil (dull surface out) to prevent overcooking of these parts, and
- covering the whole dish with plastic wrap.

Cooking fish fillet rolled is a good idea, as you can tuck in the thinner tail ends to prevent overcooking. Check fish regularly if you do not want it overcooked.

Bacon Fish Roll

Serves 6
Cooking time: 3 mins
Preparation: 15 mins
K cal: 400/serve

Ingredients
300 g (10 oz) fish fillet
20 slices Chinese bacon (lap yoke)

A
1 teaspoon honey
1 teaspoon water
dash of pepper

Preparation

Cut fish into 20 slices, each measuring 3 x 1½ cm (1¼ x ½ in). Season fish slices with ingredients A.

Place each seasoned fish slice on a slice of bacon. Roll the bacon and secure with toothpicks.

Cooking

Place bacon rolls between paper towels and microwave on power HIGH for 3 minutes.

NOTE: *Chinese bacon is belly pork marinated with soy sauce, sugar and wine and left to dry during autumn. If it is not available, substitute English bacon.*

Celery with Fish Fillet

(photo page 39)

Serves 6
Cooking time: 7 mins
Preparation: 10 mins
K cal: 130/serve

Ingredients
200 g (7 oz) fish fillet (snapper or drum)
100 g (3½ oz) celery
20 g (¾ oz) carrot
100 g(3½ oz) straw mushrooms
½ tablespoon light soy sauce

Seasoning
1 teaspoon light soy sauce
1 teaspoon wine
½ teaspoon sugar
2 teaspoons cooked oil
dash of pepper

A
1 teaspoon chopped onion
1 tablespoon oil

Preparation

Cut fish fillet into ½ cm (¼ in) thick slices and marinate with the seasoning ingredients.

Slice celery and carrot thinly.

Cooking

Combine ingredients A in a 22 cm (9 in) casserole. Microwave on power HIGH for 3 minutes, uncovered.

Stir in seasoned fish slices and straw mushrooms and microwave on power HIGH for 1 minute, uncovered.

Place sliced celery and carrot on top of fish, then spoon over the light soy sauce. Cover and microwave on power HIGH for 3 minutes.

Fish Egg Roll

(photo page 34)

Serves 6
Cooking time: 13 mins
Standing time: 10 mins
Preparation: 20 mins
K cal: 130/serve

Ingredients

**250 g (9 oz) fish fillet
(Spanish mackerel)**

A
1 tablespoon cornstarch
1 teaspoon salt
3 tablespoons water

B
4 eggs
1 teaspoon light soy sauce
dash of pepper

1 tablespoon oil
2 asparagus shoots

Dip
pineapple chili sauce

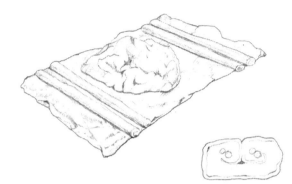

Preparation

Mince fish with ingredients A into a paste and divide into 2 portions.

Whisk ingredients B lightly and divide into 2 portions.

Cooking

Preheat a **BROWNING DISH** on power **HIGH** for 3 minutes.

Pour ½ tablespoon oil into the heated browning dish, and over this pour one portion of the B mixture. Microwave on power **HIGH** for 40 seconds to form a thin egg pancake. Repeat this process with the other portion.

Spread 1 portion of fish paste on each egg pancake. Place an asparagus shoot on top of the fish paste.

Roll up swiss roll style. Repeat this procedure with the other portion of fish paste.

Place the 2 rolls on a plate, cover with cling wrap and microwave on power **MEDIUM** for 6 minutes.

Let rolls **STAND** for 10 minutes.

Slice and serve with pineapple chili sauce.

Golden Fish Roll

Serves 6
Cooking time: 10½ mins
Preparation: 20 mins
K cal: 160/serve

Ingredients

300 g (10 oz) fish fillet (red snapper)
3 asparagus shoots
5 dried black mushrooms, soaked

A
1½ teaspoons light soy sauce
2 teaspoons cooked oil
1 teaspoon wine
1 egg white
dash of pepper

2 egg yolks, beaten
1½ cups cornflakes, crushed
2 tablespoons oil

Preparation

Cut fish into 20 slices. Pat dry with a paper towel. Season fish slices with combined ingredients A.

Cut asparagus to yield 20 pieces. Cut each softened mushroom into 4 slices.

On each seasoned fish slice, place a piece of asparagus and mushroom. Roll up the slice and secure with a toothpick. Repeat the procedure with remaining fish slices and vegetables.

Coat fish rolls with beaten egg yolk and then with crushed cornflakes.

Cooking

Preheat a **BROWNING DISH** on power **HIGH** for 7 minutes.

Pour in 2 tablespoons oil. Place fish rolls on oil and cover the dish. Give the contents a shake to ensure that rolls are coated with oil.

Remove the cover. Microwave on power **HIGH** for 3½ minutes.

Celery with Fish Fillet (p. 36), Cashew Nut Prawns (p. 49)

Golden Lily Braised Fish Head

Serves 6
Cooking time: 18½ mins
Standing time: 10 mins
Preparation: 15 mins
K cal: 160/serve

Ingredients
1 snapper or drum, 500 g
    (1 lb 1 oz)
1 teaspoon salt
3 tablespoons oil
5 slices ginger

A
20 dried golden lilies
10 red dates
10 dried black mushrooms
200 g (7 oz) hairy marrow
    vegetable
3 pieces dried sweet
    beancurd sheets (*tim
    chook*)
1½ cups water

B
12 snow peas
1 tablespoon oyster sauce
1 teaspoon light soy sauce
1½ teaspoons cornstarch
1 tablespoon water

Preparation

Clean and quarter fish head. Pat dry with a paper towel. Season with salt.

Soak dried golden lilies, red dates and dried black mushrooms to soften. Discard stone of red dates. Slice the softened black mushrooms.

Scrape off skin of hairy marrow vegetable and slice to 1 cm (½ in) thickness. Cut dried sweet beancurd sheets into strips.

Cooking

Preheat a BROWNING DISH on power HIGH for 8 minutes. Add oil, ginger slices and seasoned fish head. Microwave on power HIGH for 2 minutes, uncovered.

Add ingredients A, cover and microwave on power HIGH for 7 minutes. Add combined ingredients B and microwave on power HIGH for 1½ minutes, uncovered.

Cover the dish and let it STAND for 10 minutes.

NOTE: *Golden lilies are flowers grown in the highlands. Plucked when dried, they give a distinctive flavor to your cooking.*

Good Things Come Your Way!

Serves 10
Cooking time: 7½ mins
Preparation: 20 mins
K cal: 70/serve

Ingredients
12 pieces dried oysters
10 g (⅓ oz) black moss
    seaweed
3 whole Taiwanese cabbages

A
300 g (10 oz) fish fillet
    (Spanish mackerel)
1 teaspoon salt
3 tablespoons water
1 tablespoon cornstarch

Gravy
1 cup dried oyster water
1 teaspoon wine
½ teaspoon ginger juice
1 teaspoon honey
1 teaspoon salt
1 teaspoon cornstarch

Preparation

Soak dried oysters in 1 cup water. Retain water for gravy. Soak black moss seaweed and discard water.

Halve Taiwanese cabbages lengthwise and place them on a plate with leaves facing the center of the plate.

Mince ingredients A into a paste. Mix in one-third of the black moss seaweed. Divide mixture into 12 portions.

Flatten each portion of the fish paste. Spread a little seaweed and place 1 softened oyster on it. Gather edges of the fish paste to enclose the filling and mold paste into an oval shape.

Place fish ovals on top of the Taiwanese cabbage in the plate. Cover the plate with cling wrap.

Cooking

Microwave fish ovals on power MEDIUM for 5 minutes.

Combine gravy ingredients in a small casserole and microwave on power HIGH for 2½ minutes, uncovered. Pour cooked gravy over the fish ovals and serve.

NOTE: *This Chinese New Year fare goes by the name Hoe See Fatt Choy. To the Cantonese, hoe see means dried oysters and fatt choy, black moss seaweed. The Cantonese words also sound like 'good things' (hoe see), 'good luck' (fatt choy). May good things come your way!*

Koong Poh Tong Sut

(photo page 43)

Serves 6
Cooking time: 8 mins
Preparation: 15 mins
K cal: 95/serve

Ingredients
250 g (9 oz) catfish fillet
100 g (3½ oz) onion

A
1½ teaspoons chopped
    garlic
8 g (¼ oz) dried chiles,
    soaked
1 teaspoon chopped ginger
1½ tablespoons oil

B
1 tablespoon oyster sauce
1½ teaspoons wine
1½ teaspoons sugar
1 teaspoon dark soy sauce
1 teaspoon light soy sauce

Preparation

Slice catfish fillet thinly. Cut onion into wedges.

Cooking

Combine ingredients A in a 2 liter (2 qt) shallow casserole and microwave on power HIGH for 4 minutes, uncovered.

Add ingredients B and microwave on power HIGH for 1 minute, uncovered.

Stir in fish slices and onions and microwave on power HIGH for 3 minutes, uncovered.

Silver and Golden Fish

Serves 6
Cooking time: 13½ mins
Preparation: 10 mins
K cal: 140/serve

Ingredients
1 pompano, 350 g (12 oz)
3 tablespoons oil

Gravy A
1 teaspoon honey or sugar
2 teaspoons light soy sauce
1 teaspoon sesame oil
¼ cup water
1 teaspoon ginger juice

Gravy B
1½ teaspoons preserved
    soybean paste
1 red chile, chopped
4 cloves garlic, chopped
1 teaspoon sugar
3 tablespoons water

Garnish
spring onion and Chinese parsley

Preparation
Clean and gut the fish, then pat dry with a paper towel.

Cooking
Cook gravy A: combine ingredients A in a small casserole and microwave on power HIGH for 1½ minutes, uncovered.

Pour cooked gravy A on a serving plate.

Preheat a BROWNING DISH on power HIGH for 8 minutes. Spoon in oil, add the fish, cover and microwave on power HIGH for 3 minutes.

Remove fried fish and place it fried side up on gravy A in the serving plate.

Cook gravy B: Retain ½ tablespoon oil in the browning dish. Add soybean paste and chopped chile and garlic. Microwave on power HIGH for 1½ minutes, uncovered. Pour in remaining ingredients B and microwave on power HIGH for 1 minute, uncovered.

Pour cooked gravy B over fried fish and serve garnished with spring onion and Chinese parsley.

Spicy Sauce Steamed Fish

Serves 6
Cooking time: 9 mins
Standing time: 5 mins
Preparation: 10 mins
K cal: 135/serve

Ingredients
1 freshwater fish, 350 g (12 oz)

A
1 red chile
4 shallots
4 cloves garlic
50 g (1½ oz) pork fat
1 teaspoon oil

B
2 teaspoons preserved
    soybean paste
1 tablespoon oyster sauce
½ tablespoon sugar
¼ cup water

Garnish
finely sliced lettuce

Preparation
Clean and gut fish. Finely chop red chile, shallots and garlic.

Cooking
Combine ingredients A in a 20 cm (8 in) casserole. Microwave on power HIGH for 4 minutes, uncovered. Add ingredients B and microwave on power HIGH for 1½ minutes, uncovered.

Place fish in an oval casserole. Pour cooked gravy over fish and cover casserole. Microwave on power MEDIUM for 3½ minutes.

Let dish STAND for 5 minutes. Garnish with lettuce.

NOTE: *For this recipe, any freshwater fish may be used. The author prefers 'feh chow yee', which is found in Malayan and African waters (feh chow is Cantonese for Africa).*

Koong Poh Tong Sut (p. 41), Spicy Asparagus (p. 141)

Steamed Fish with Ham

Serves 6
Cooking time: 4½ mins
Preparation: 15 mins
K cal: 160/serve

Ingredients
300 g (10 oz) fish fillet
    (pompano)
3 slices ham
6 dried black mushrooms,
    soaked
100 g (3½ oz) Tientsin
    cabbage (leaves only)

A
1 tablespoon cooked oil
½ teaspoon sugar
1 teaspoon ginger juice
dash of pepper

Gravy
2 teaspoons light soy sauce
1 teaspoon wine
1 teaspoon sesame oil
½ cup water
1 teaspoon honey

Preparation

Cut fish fillet into 18 slices. Season fish with ingredients A.

Cut each ham slice into 6 pieces. Cut each softened mushroom into 3 slices.

Place cabbage leaves on an oval plate. Arrange seasoned fish slices, alternating with ham and mushroom slices, in 2 rows on the cabbage.

Combine gravy ingredients and pour over the fish.

Cooking

Cover the contents of the plate with cling wrap and microwave on power MEDIUM for 4½ minutes.

Steamed Teochew Fish

Serves 6
Cooking time: 8½ mins
Standing time: 5 mins
Preparation: 10 mins
K cal: 175/serve

Ingredients
1 pompano, 350 g (12 oz)
50 g (2 oz) salted mustard
    cabbage
100 g (3½ oz) belly pork
4 dried black mushrooms,
    soaked
1 red chile
1 tomato
1 soft white beancurd
    square (suey tau foo)

A
1 teaspoon chopped garlic
½ teaspoon oil

B
¼ cup water
1 teaspoon sugar
1 teaspoon light soy sauce

Preparation

Clean and gut the fish. Slice salted mustard cabbage, belly pork, softened black mushrooms, red chile and tomato.

Cut beancurd square into quarters.

Cooking

Combine ingredients A with salted mustard cabbage and belly pork in a 20 cm (8 in) casserole. Microwave on power HIGH for 3½ minutes, uncovered.

Add ingredients B, mushrooms and chile, and microwave on power HIGH for 2 minutes, uncovered.

Place fish, tomato and beancurd in an oval casserole and pour cooked ingredients over the fish.

Cover the casserole and microwave on power MEDIUM for 3 minutes.

Let the dish STAND for 5 minutes.

NOTE: *If using other varieties of fish where the body is thick, fillet the fish by cutting from the stomach to the central bone on either side of the bone. Remove the bone. Spread both sides of fillet on the plate for cooking.*

Stuffed Red Snapper

Serves 6
Cooking time: 7 mins
Preparation: 15 mins
K cal: 45/serve

Ingredients
1 red snapper, 400 g (14 oz)

A
100 g (3½ oz) shrimp
20 g (1 oz) carrot
20 g (1 oz) water chestnuts
1 teaspoon salt
¼ teaspoon sugar
dash of pepper

Gravy
1 tablespoon oyster sauce
½ cup water
1 teaspoon cornstarch

Preparation

Clean and gut the fish. Slit it from belly to tail. Spread fish open and scrape off meat, leaving the skin and bone still attached to the head.

Chop fish meat together with ingredients A till fine.

Place chopped mixture on both sides of the fish bone, cover with the skin and pat back into the fish shape.

Place stuffed fish in an oval casserole.

Cooking

Combine gravy ingredients in a small casserole and microwave on power **HIGH** for 1 minute, uncovered.

Pour gravy over the fish. Cover and microwave on power **MEDIUM-HIGH** for 6 minutes.

NOTE: *If water chestnuts are not available, substitute 20 g (1 oz) sweet apple or pear.*

PRAWNS

The texture and flavor of prawns are equally important. Fresh prawns have a crunchy texture, while stale prawns break like sawdust in the mouth. Fresh prawns have glossy shells and on really fresh prawns these are difficult to remove; heads are firmly attached to the body and there is no unpleasant fishy smell.

Freeze prawns in single or thin layers if you plan to use the microwave oven to defrost. It is never safe to refreeze foods, and seafood particularly is easily spoiled, so always freeze in small portions, sufficient for single meals.

Recipes specify sizes and where they do not, use medium-sized prawns. Shrimp or very small prawns are the ideal choice for mincing and medium-sized prawns are sweetest for steaming, tiger prawns being best for this cooking method.

To remove the seafood odor from the oven after cooking, heat a cup of water with a wedge of lemon and some cloves in it.

Bacon Prawns (p. 48), Salad Cup (p. 135)

Bacon Prawns

(photo page 47)

Serves 3
Cooking time: 11 mins
Preparation: 10 mins
K cal: 390/serve

Ingredients
6 large prawns, 400 g (14 oz)
½ teaspoon sugar
dash of pepper
3 sprigs Chinese parsley, cut in half
6 slices Chinese bacon (*lap yoke*)

Preparation

Shell and devein prawns. Score crosswise at center. Pat prawns dry with paper towels.

Season prawns with sugar and pepper.

Place half a sprig of Chinese parsley on each prawn, wrap Chinese bacon around the prawn and secure with a toothpick.

Cooking

Preheat a BROWNING DISH on power HIGH for 8 minutes.

Place prepared prawns in the browning dish, stir prawns and microwave on power HIGH for 3 minutes, uncovered.

Black Bean Prawns

Serves 6
Cooking time: 7 mins
Preparation: 10 mins
K cal: 70/serve

Ingredients
18 prawns, 400 g (14 oz)

A
½ egg white
¼ teaspoon sugar

B
1 tablespoon salted black beans
1 teaspoon chopped garlic
1 teaspoon chopped ginger
1 tablespoon oil

80 g (3 oz) carrot slices
10 g (⅓ oz) snow peas
½ teaspoon sugar

Preparation

Remove head, tail and shell, then devein prawns. Pat dry with paper towels. Season prawns with ingredients A.

Cooking

Combine ingredients B in a 22 cm (9 in) casserole and microwave on power HIGH for 3½ minutes, uncovered.

Stir in seasoned prawns, carrot slices, snow peas and sugar. Microwave on power HIGH for 3½ minutes, uncovered. Stir halfway through the cooking cycle.

Cashew Nut Prawns

(photo page 39)

Serves 8
Cooking time: 7 mins
Preparation: 10 mins
K cal: 90/serve

Ingredients
24 prawns, 500 g (1 lb 1 oz)

A
½ egg white
¼ teaspoon sugar
¼ teaspoon salt

B
6 dried chiles
1½ teaspoons chopped
    garlic
1 tablespoon oil

C
1 teaspoon Chinese barbe-
    cue sauce (*tim cheong*)
1 teaspoon oyster sauce
1 teaspoon light soy sauce
½ teaspoon sugar

Garnish

50 g (2 oz) roasted cashew nuts
chopped Chinese parsley

Preparation

Remove head, tail and shell, then devein prawns. Pat dry with paper towels. Season prawns with combined ingredients A.

Cooking

Combine ingredients B in a 22 cm (9 in) casserole and microwave on power HIGH for 3½ minutes, uncovered.

Add combined ingredients C and microwave on power HIGH for 1 minute.

Add seasoned prawns and microwave on power HIGH for 2½ minutes.

Garnish with roasted cashew nuts and Chinese parsley.

Claypot Drunken Prawns

Serves 2
Cooking time: 13 mins
Preparation: 10 mins
K cal: 185/serve

Ingredients
6 freshwater prawns, 300 g
    (10 oz)

A
10 g (⅓ oz) ginger
1 teaspoon chopped garlic
1 tablespoon oil

B
5 cups water
1½ teaspoons salt
1 teaspoon sugar

3 tablespoons rice wine

Preparation

Clean prawns and halve them lengthwise, leaving shell, head and tail intact. Pat dry with paper towel.

Cooking

Combine ingredients A in a 26 cm (20 in) claypot and microwave till fragrant on power HIGH for 3 minutes, uncovered.

Add ingredients B and prawns. Cover and cook on power HIGH for 10 minutes.

Add the wine and cover the claypot. Let it STAND for 5 minutes.

NOTE: *The dish is traditionally cooked in a claypot, but it is equally good in a casserole.*

Goldfish Prawns (p. 51), Four Seasons with Scallops (p. 131)

Goldfish Prawns

(photo page 50)

Serves 6
Cooking time: 6 mins
Preparation: 15 mins
K cal: 40/serve

Ingredients

300 g (10 oz) shrimp
1 egg white
1 teaspoon salt
1 teaspoon sugar
1 teaspoon wine
dash of pepper

10 medium-sized Chinese
 soup spoons

1 carrot
20 green peas (for fish eyes)

Preparation

Shell and devein shrimp. Mince all ingredients except green peas and carrot into a paste and divide into 10 portions.

Grease Chinese soup spoons. Place each portion of the shrimp paste in a soup spoon and shape it to resemble goldfish body.

Halve carrot lengthwise and slice thinly, on the diagonal, for fish fins. Trim a little off the edge (see diagram).

Complete the goldfish with green pea eyes and sliced carrot fins.

Cooking

Place the prepared spoons on a large plate. Cover with cling wrap and microwave on power **MEDIUM** for 6 minutes.

Remove from spoons and serve on a bed of sliced lettuce.

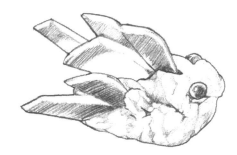

Prawns with Hot Sauce

Serves 4
Cooking time: 7 mins
Preparation: 10 mins
K cal: 170/serve

Ingredients
12 prawns, 600 g (1 lb 5 oz)

A
20 g (1 oz) shallots
30 g (1 oz) red chiles
1 teaspoon preserved soy
    beans
¼ piece red fermented
    beancurd (*nam yee*)
2 cloves garlic
2 sprigs Chinese parsley

1 tablespoon oyster sauce
1 teaspoon sugar
2 tablespoons oil
2 tablespoons water

Preparation

Remove head and shell of prawns, leaving the tail intact. Make a slit lengthwise down the back of the prawns. Then make a cut 1 cm (½ in) wide right through the center of the prawn.

Turn the tail through the 1 cm (½ in) slit. Pat prawns dry with paper towels.

Blend ingredients A into a paste.

Cooking

Combine blended ingredients A with oyster sauce, sugar and oil in a 20 cm (8 in) casserole.

Microwave on power HIGH for 3½ minutes, uncovered.

Add water and prawns. Cover and microwave on power HIGH for 3½ minutes.

Screwpine Leaf Prawns

(photo page 55)

Serves 4
Cooking time: 13½ mins
Preparation: 10 mins
K cal: 200/serve

Ingredients
12 prawns, 400 g (14 oz)
½ teaspoon salt

A
30 g (1 oz) shallots
50 g (1½ oz) red chiles
4 cloves garlic
½ teaspoon sugar
30 g (1 oz) dried prawns,
   soaked

3 tablespoons oil
12 screwpine leaves
12 toothpicks

Preparation

Wash prawns, slit opening at the back and pat dry with paper towels. Season with salt.

Chop ingredients A finely.

Cooking

Combine chopped ingredients A with 1½ tablespoons oil in a 16 cm (6 in) casserole and microwave on power HIGH for 3 minutes.

Stuff cooked ingredients in the slit of the prawns. Bind prawns with screwpine leaves, securing with a cocktail stick.

Preheat a BROWNING DISH on power HIGH for 6 minutes. Add 1½ tablespoons oil and heat for a further 30 seconds.

Place prawns in the browning dish and microwave on power HIGH for 4 minutes. Turn prawns over after 2 minutes of the cooking cycle.

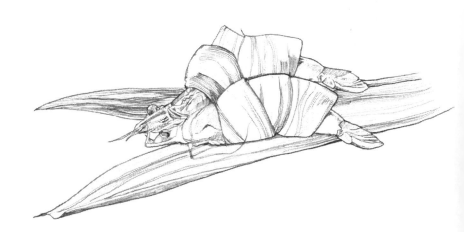

Stuffed Freshwater Prawns (p. 57)

Screwpine Leaf Prawns (p. 53), Stuffed Eggplant (p. 143)

Sizzling Prawns

Serves 6
Cooking time: 12 mins
Standing time: 5–10 mins
Preparation: 10 mins
K cal: 60/serve

Ingredients
18 prawns, 400 g (14 oz)

A
1/8 teaspoon baking soda
1/2 teaspoon sugar
1/2 teaspoon salt
dash of pepper

B
1/2 tablespoon chopped
    onion
1/2 tablespoon oil

C
1/2 tablespoon oyster sauce
1/4 teaspoon dark soy sauce
1/2 tablespoon Chinese barbecue sauce (*tim cheong*)
1/4 cup water
1/2 teaspoon wine

1/2 tablespoon oil

Preparation

Shell and devein prawns, leaving tails intact, and pat dry with paper towels. Combine ingredients A and season prawns with it.

Cooking

Combine ingredients B in a small casserole and microwave on power HIGH for 2 1/2 minutes, uncovered.

Add combined ingredients C and microwave on power HIGH for 1 1/2 minutes. Leave the gravy mixture aside.

Preheat a BROWNING DISH on power HIGH for 8 minutes. Place oil and seasoned prawns in the browning dish and stir prawns.

Pour gravy mixture over the prawns, cover the browning dish and let it STAND for 5–10 minutes.

Steamed Prawns

Serves 8
Cooking time: 4/2 mins
Preparation: 10 mins
K cal: 35/serve

Ingredients
24 tiger prawns, 500 g (1 lb
    1 oz)
1/2 teaspoon salt

A
2 teaspoons wine
1 teaspoon ginger juice
2 teaspoons light soy sauce
1/2 teaspoon sugar
1/3 cup water

Garnish
spring onions and Chinese
    parsley, cut into 4 cm
      (1 1/2 in) lengths

Preparation

Wash prawns, pat dry with paper towels and season with salt. Cut opening at the back, score crosswise at center, leaving head and tail intact.

Arrange prawns in a circle with the head facing the edge of a 32 cm (12 1/2 in) plate.

Cooking

Combine ingredients A and pour over the prawns. Cover the whole plate with cling wrap. Microwave on power MEDIUM-HIGH for 4 1/2 minutes.

Garnish with spring onions and Chinese parsley.

Stuffed Freshwater Prawns

(photo page 54)

Serves 5
Cooking time: 10 mins
Preparation: 10 mins
K cal: 120/serve

Ingredients
**10 freshwater prawns, 800 g
(1 lb 12 oz)**

A
**40 g (1½ oz) water chest-
nuts**
30 g (1 oz) carrot
2 sprigs Chinese parsley
½ egg white
½ teaspoon salt
¼ teaspoon pepper

50 g (1½ oz) green peas
oil for basting

Preparation

Wash prawns and slit opening lengthwise from the back. Devein.
Remove the meat but leave head and tail intact.

Chop prawn meat with ingredients A, and mix in green peas. Stuff
chopped ingredients into the prawn shell.

Arrange prawns in a circle with prawn head facing edge of a 32 cm
(12½ in) plate.

Baste the stuffed prawns with oil.

Cooking

Microwave on power **HIGH** for 10 minutes, uncovered. Baste prawns
with oil every 3 minutes of the cooking cycle.

CRAB & MUSSELS

Two species of crab popularly used in Chinese recipes are the mud and flower crabs. The latter is a deep-sea crab that has plenty of easily extracted meat. Since it is not very tasty on its own, it is best cooked with spices; its meat is often added to sharksfin soup. The mud crab, on the other hand, is steamed for its sweeter meat.

When buying, choose male crabs, which have more meat. To differentiate male and female crabs, look for the belly flap: the male has a narrow flap and the female a rounded, broader one that ends in a point. Crab roe, naturally, is present only in female crabs. The same applies to mud crabs.

Another way to choose meaty crabs is to apply pressure on the belly flap of mud crabs: if it is hard and spongy then it will contain plenty of meat. Press both ends of the shell of flower crabs: if the shell does not break, the crab is meaty.

If you have to cut crabs, first remove the pincers. Lift the belly flap and twist it off, then separate the hard shell from the body. Wash thoroughly and cut according to recipe requirements.

Mussels can be cooked in their own shells. Simply place them on the outer edge of a round plate.

Steamed Crabs (p. 60), Watercress with Fresh Oysters (p. 146)

Steamed Crabs

(photo page 59)

Serves 4
Cooking time: 5 mins
Preparation: 15 mins
K cal: 60/serve

Ingredients
4 crabs, 500 g (1 lb 1½ oz)

A
3 teaspoons ginger juice
3 teaspoons wine
1 tablespoon light soy sauce
1 teaspoon sugar
¼ cup water

Garnish
spring onion and Chinese
    parsley, cut to 2 cm (1
    in) lengths

Preparation

Clean crabs and cut into quarters. Crack shell of claws.

Cooking

Place crabs in a 2 liter (2 qt) shallow casserole. Pour combined ingredients A over the crabs, cover and microwave on power HIGH for 5 minutes.

Sprinkle on spring onion and Chinese parsley and serve immediately.

NOTE: *In order to yield the best flavor in food that calls for steaming, especially seafood, it has to be fresh, and if possible alive just before cooking. For this recipe, use live crabs.*

Sweet Sour Crabs

(photo page 152)

Serves 4
Cooking time: 9 mins
Preparation: 20 mins
K cal: 135/serve

Ingredients
4 crabs, 400 g (14 oz)
1 egg, beaten

A
50 g (1½ oz) pickled spring
    garlic
30 g (1 oz) pickled ginger
20 g (½ oz) red chiles
1½ teaspoons cornstarch
½ cup water

B
1½ teaspoons chopped
    garlic
1½ tablespoons oil

Preparation

Clean crabs and cut body into quarters. Crack shell of claws.

Slice pickled spring garlic and ginger finely. Remove seeds from chiles and slice finely.

Mix cornstarch with ½ cup water.

Cooking

Combine ingredients B in a 4 liter (7 pt) casserole and microwave on power HIGH for 3½ minutes, uncovered.

Add crabs with combined ingredients A. Cover and microwave on power HIGH for 5½ minutes.

Let the dish STAND for 5 minutes before serving.

NOTE: *Pickled spring garlic and pickled ginger are often used to cook sweet and sour recipes. They have to be thinly sliced or shredded to give the correct texture as well as taste.*

Tomato Crabs

Serves 4
Cooking time: 10 mins
Preparation: 20 mins
K cal: 140/serve

Ingredients
4 crabs, 500 g (1 lb 1 oz)
80 g (3 oz) tomato

A
50 g (1½ oz) onion
1½ tablespoons oil

B
1½ tablespoons tomato
    sauce
1 tablespoon oyster sauce
1 teaspoon sugar
¼ cup water

1 egg, beaten

Garnish
spring onion and Chinese
    parsley, chopped finely

Preparation

Clean crabs and cut into quarters. Crack shell of claws.

Cut tomato into wedges. Chop onion coarsely.

Cooking

Combine ingredients A in a 2 liter (2 qt) shallow casserole. Microwave on power HIGH for 4 minutes, uncovered.

Add crabs, tomato and combined ingredients B. Cover and microwave on power HIGH for 6 minutes.

Immediately after the cooking cycle, stir in beaten egg, cover and let STAND for 10 minutes.

Sprinkle with chopped spring onion and Chinese parsley.

Soybean Mussels

Serves 6
Cooking time: 8½ mins
Preparation: 15 mins
K cal: 60/serve

Ingredients
400 g (14 oz) mussels, thin-
    shell variety

A
2 teaspoons preserved soy
    beans
5 cloves garlic
10 g (⅓ oz) red chiles
1½ tablespoons oil

3 tablespoons water

Preparation

Wash mussels under running water.

Mince together preserved soy beans, garlic and red chiles.

Cooking

Combine ingredients A in a 2 liter (2 qt) shallow casserole and microwave on power HIGH for 4 minutes, uncovered.

Add mussels and water. Cover and microwave on power MEDIUM for 4½ minutes. Stir after 2 minutes of the cooking cycle.

NOTE: *If fresh mussels in shell are not available, use frozen mussels. Defrost for 2½ minutes, and change cooking time to 2–2½ minutes.*

Spicy Barbecued Spare Ribs (p. 68), Fried Noodles (Char Cheong Meen, p. 156)

PORK

As may be seen from the recipe list below, all parts of the pig are used in Chinese cooking. When shopping, remember some basic facts about buying pork:

- fillet, the most tender part, is used for traditionally stir-fried dishes,
- fore legs have a higher meat content than hind legs,
- topside meat is ideal for mincing as it has a small portion of fat, which makes the mince smoother,
- ribs are divided into hard bones (for soups) and the meatier soft bones for steaming, and
- belly cuts are streaked with fat and excellent for roasting.

As with all meats, cut against the grain.

Buy fresh meat that is reddish, glossy and moist. Freeze single meal portions and try not to keep pork in the freezer for more than three weeks as it dehydrates the meat. Label packages of pork to indicate date frozen and cut of meat.

Standing time is important when roasting large portions. The meat is taken out of the oven before it is done, then wrapped in foil (dull side out). The temperature rises within and finishes the cooking.

Black Bean Spare Ribs

(photo page 140)

Serves 6
Cooking time: 11½ mins
Preparation: 5 mins
K cal: 240/serve

Ingredients
600 g (1 lb 5 oz) spare ribs
1 red chile

A
2 teaspoons chopped garlic
1 tablespoon oil

B
**2 tablespoons salted black
beans**
1½ teaspoons sugar
1 teaspoon wine
¼ cup water

Preparation

Cut spare ribs to bite size. Slice the red chile.

Cooking

Combine ingredients A in a 22 cm (9 in) casserole and microwave on power HIGH for 3½ minutes, uncovered.

Add ingredients B, then cover and microwave on power HIGH for 1½ minutes.

Add spare ribs and chile slices and leave spare ribs to marinate in the cooked ingredients for 30 minutes.

Cover the casserole and microwave on power MEDIUM for 6½ minutes.

NOTE: *This is sometimes served in tiny sauce plates as a dish for dim sum, literally 'small eats', a lunchtime favorite.*

Black Vinegar Pig's Feet

Serves 6
Cooking time: 55½ minutes
Preparation: 10 mins
K cal: 380/serve

Ingredients
1 kg (2 lb 3 oz) pig's feet
2¾ cups black vinegar
300 g (10½ oz) ginger
1 tablespoon sesame oil
300 g (10½ oz) brown sugar

Preparation

Ask your butcher to cut pig's feet into pieces. Remove any bristles and clean pig's feet thoroughly.

Marinate pig's feet in ½ cup black vinegar for 1 hour.

Scrape skin off ginger and crush with the flat of a chopper.

Cooking

Combine ginger and sesame oil in a 5 liter (5 qt) casserole and microwave on power HIGH for 4 minutes, uncovered.

Add remaining ingredients, then cover and microwave on power HIGH for 6½ minutes. Next, simmer on power MEDIUM-LOW for 45 minutes, still covered.

Allow meat and ginger to mature for 1 day before heating to serve.

NOTE: *This dish makes its appearance during the confinement period after childbirth. It is believed to help shrink the uterus and expel 'wind'.*

Claypot Spicy Spare Ribs

(photo page 116)

Serves 6
Cooking time: 19 mins
Preparation: 15 mins
K cal: 215/serve

Ingredients

500 g (1 lb 1 oz) spare ribs
1 tablespoon cornstarch
2 tablespoons water

A
5 dried chiles
2 star anise
**4 cm (1½ in) cinnamon
    stick**
**½ tablespoon chopped
    ginger**
1½ tablespoons oil

B
1 tablespoon oyster sauce
2 teaspoons dark soy sauce
2 teaspoons wine
1 teaspoon salt
¼ cup water

Preparation

Ask your butcher to cut spare ribs into serving pieces. Mix cornstarch with 2 tablespoons water.

Wash dried chiles and soak to soften. Combine ingredients B.

Cooking

Combine ingredients A in a 3 liter (3 qt) claypot and microwave on power HIGH for 4 minutes, uncovered.

Add ingredients B and spare ribs and microwave on power HIGH for 5 minutes.

Stir in the cornstarch mixture and microwave on power MEDIUM for 10 minutes. Stir every 2 minutes of the cooking cycle. The claypot remains uncovered throughout.

Hong Kong Char Siew

Serves 10
Cooking time: 12 mins
Preparation: 10 mins
K cal: 500/serve

Ingredients

1 kg (2 lb 3 oz) belly pork

A
1 teaspoon garlic paste
**3 tablespoons black *hoisin*
    sauce**
1 tablespoon oyster sauce
2 teaspoons wine
1½ teaspoons sugar
1½ teaspoons sesame oil
**1 piece red fermented
    beancurd (*nam yee*)**

1 tablespoon oil

Preparation

Cut belly pork into 3 long strips. Marinate pork strips in combined ingredients A for 5 hours or overnight.

Garlic paste is obtained by pounding garlic.

Cooking

Preheat a BROWNING DISH on power HIGH for 8 minutes. Pour in oil and place seasoned pork strips on oil to cook.

Turn pork strips over and microwave on power HIGH for 4 minutes, uncovered.

Slice Char Siew into bite-sized pieces before serving.

NOTE: *Char Siew may be served as a main dish, as an ingredient in other recipes, for example fried rice, or as an hors d'oeuvre for drinkers.*

Kow Yoke

Serves 6
Cooking time: 41½ mins
Standing time: 10 mins
Preparation: 10 mins
K cal: 400/serve

Ingredients
300 g (10 oz) roasted belly pork

A
300 g (10 oz) yam
1½ teaspoons chopped garlic
1½ tablespoons oil

B
1½ pieces red fermented beancurd (*nam yee*)
1 tablespoon red *hoisin* sauce
1 teaspoon sugar
1½ teaspoons wine
1 cup water

Preparation

Cut roasted belly pork into 1 cm (½ in) thick slices. Peel skin off yam and cut yam into 1 cm (½ in) thick pieces. Combine ingredients B.

Cooking

Combine ingredients A in an 18 cm (7 in) casserole and microwave on power HIGH for 5 minutes, uncovered. Remove yam and keep aside.

Pour ingredients B into the same casserole and microwave on power HIGH for 1½ minutes, uncovered. Set aside gravy.

In a 24 cm (9 in) casserole, arrange roasted pork pieces, skin down, alternating with a piece of yam until the yam and pork are used up.

Pour cooked gravy over the arrangement and cover meat and yam with aluminium foil, dull surface out. (Note that the foil covers only the food, not the entire casserole, to prevent it from drying out.) Microwave on power MEDIUM-LOW for 35 minutes, covered in this way.

Let the dish STAND for 10 minutes before serving.

NOTE: *This traditional Hakka recipe is served at all festive seasons and grand occasions such as wedding dinners. It is served in generous thick slices.*

Pork with Szechuan Vegetable

Serves 6
Cooking time: 11½ mins
Preparation: 10 mins
K cal: 155/serve

Ingredients
150 g (5 oz) Szechuan vegetable
A
150 g (5 oz) belly pork
1½ teaspoons chopped garlic
1 tablespoon oil

1½ teaspoons sugar
½ cup water

Preparation

Wash and cut Szechuan vegetable and belly pork into strips.

Cooking

Wrap Szechuan vegetable strips with paper towels and microwave on power HIGH for 2½ minutes to dry.

Combine ingredients A in a 22 cm (9 in) casserole and microwave on power HIGH for 4½ minutes, uncovered.

Add remaining ingredients. Cover and microwave on power HIGH for 4½ minutes.

Wang Choy Chow Sow (p. 69), Winter Delight (p. 147)

Sizzling Liver

(photo page 121)

Serves 4
Cooking time: 12½ mins
Standing time: 10 mins
Preparation: 10 mins
K cal: 125/serve

Ingredients
200 g (7 oz) pig's liver
80 g (3 oz) spring onion

A
100 g (3½ oz) young ginger
1½ teaspoons chopped
garlic
1 tablespoon oil

B
1 tablespoon oyster sauce
⅓ cup water
1 teaspoon wine

Preparation

Slice liver thinly. Wash and cut spring onion into 2 cm (1 in) lengths. Slice ginger thinly.

Cooking

Combine ingredients A in a 16 cm (6 in) casserole and microwave on power HIGH for 3½ minutes, uncovered.

Add ingredients B and microwave on power HIGH for 1 minute. Set aside the cooked mixture.

Preheat a BROWNING DISH on power HIGH for 8 minutes. Pour in cooked gravy mixture and liver, place spring onions on top of the liver and cover the browning dish.

Let Sizzling Liver STAND for 10 minutes to finish cooking.

Spicy Barbecued Spare Ribs

(photo page 62)

Serves 6
Cooking time: 13 mins
Preparation: 10 mins
K cal: 215/serve

Ingredients
500 g (1 lb 1 oz) meaty
spare ribs

A
2 pieces red fermented
beancurd (*nam yee*)
1 tablespoon sugar
2 teaspoons wine
1 teaspoon sesame oil
1 teaspoon garlic paste
1½ teaspoons pepper
1 tablespoon red *hoisin*
sauce

1 tablespoon oil

Preparation

Cut spare ribs to bite-sized pieces and pat dry with paper towels. Marinate them overnight in combined ingredients A.

Cooking

Preheat a BROWNING DISH on power HIGH for 8 minutes. Pour in oil and add the seasoned spare ribs to microwave on power HIGH for 5 minutes, uncovered.

Turn the spare ribs after 2 minutes of the cooking cycle.

NOTE: *Nam Yee Pai Kuat Wong is the Cantonese name for this dish, which is ideal for a buffet party since it can be prepared a day in advance. It tastes exactly like barbecued spare ribs.*

Tai Khut Tai Lei

Serves 6
Cooking time: 7 mins
Preparation: 15 mins
K cal: 130/serve

Ingredients
250 g (9 oz) pig's tongue
80 g (3 oz) spring garlic

A
20 g (¾ oz) candied orange
1 teaspoon chopped garlic
1½ tablespoons oil

B
¼ cup chicken stock
1 tablespoon oyster sauce
1 teaspoon cornstarch

50 g (2 oz) snow peas

Preparation

Clean pig's tongue and slice thinly. Cut spring garlic into 3 cm (1 in) lengths. Shred candied orange.

Combine ingredients B.

Cooking

Combine ingredients A in a 2 liter (2 qt) shallow casserole and microwave on power HIGH for 3 minutes, uncovered.

Add pig's tongue and spring garlic. Cover and microwave on power HIGH for 2 minutes.

Add combined ingredients B and snow peas, stir and cover. Microwave on power HIGH for 2 minutes.

Wang Choy Chow Sow

(photo page 67)

Serves 10
Cooking time: 1 hr 6 mins
Standing time: 15 mins
Preparation: 20 mins
K cal: 190/serve

Ingredients
2 roasted pig's forelegs,
**   about 1½ kg (3 lb 5 oz)**
2 tablespoons cornstarch
3 tablespoons water

A
25 g (1 oz) dried scallops
1 piece pig's spleen (*chee wang lei*)
10 small dried black mushrooms
15 g (½ oz) red dates
10 g (⅓ oz) black moss seaweed, soaked

B
2¼ cups water
2 teaspoons wine
2 tablespoons oyster sauce

Preparation

Trim off bone from the roasted pig's forelegs. Mix cornstarch with 3 tablespoons water.

Break dried scallops into pieces. Cut *chee wang lei* in half. Soak dried black mushrooms to soften and discard water. Soak red dates and remove the stones.

Divide ingredients A into 2 portions. Stuff one portion into each roasted foreleg and secure with string.

Cooking

Place stuffed pig's forelegs in a 5 liter (5 qt) casserole. Pour combined ingredients B over the stuffed forelegs. Cover the casserole and microwave on power HIGH for 6 minutes.

Simmer on power MEDIUM-LOW for 1 hour, covered. Turn stuffed forelegs over halfway through the cooking cycle.

Immediately after the cooking cycle, add the cornstarch mixture, wrap the whole casserole with aluminium foil and let it STAND for 15 minutes.

Slice into 1 cm (½ in) thick slices and place on a large serving plate. Pour gravy over the meat.

NOTE: *This is a Chinese New Year dish to wish diners a Host of Unexpected Riches. Wishing you Wang Choy Chow Sow.*

Yuen Thai (Braised Pork, p. 71), Beansprouts with Saltfish (p. 122)

Yuen Thai (Braised Pork)

(photo page 70)

Serves 6
Cooking time: 50 mins
Standing time: 15 mins
Preparation: 10 mins
K cal: 800/serve

Ingredients

1 kg (2 lb 3 oz) shoulder
    pork, with skin
2½ teaspoons cornstarch
2 tablespoons water

A
1½ teaspoons chopped
    garlic
1 piece red fermented
    beancurd (*nam yee*)
1 tablespoon oil

B
1 teaspoon Szechuan
    pepper
2 star anise
5 cloves
½ teaspoon five-spice
    powder
1 teaspoon wine
1½ teaspoons dark soy
    sauce
1½ cups water
2 cm (¾ in) cinnamon stick

Preparation

Clean shoulder pork and remove any bristles. Mix cornstarch with 2 tablespoons water.

Cooking

Combine ingredients A in a deep 24 cm (9 in) casserole and microwave on power HIGH for 2 minutes, uncovered.

Add ingredients B, mix evenly and put in the shoulder pork, skin side down. Cover and microwave on power HIGH for 8 minutes.

Simmer on power MEDIUM-LOW for 40 minutes, still covered. Baste with gravy after every 10 minutes of the cooking cycle to ensure that the meat does not dry out.

Immediately at the end of the cooking cycle, stir in cornstarch mixture and let pork STAND for 15 minutes, covered.

Slice Yuen Thai into 1 cm (½ in) thick slices, arrange on a flat dish and pour gravy over the slices.

BEEF

Beef is not a popular meat among Chinese, partly for religious reasons. It is not served during the Chinese New Year's Eve reunion dinner or on the first day of the Chinese New Year, nor is it sold for a few weeks in that period in China.

The muscle is normally divided by thin layers of tissue. To aid fast cooking, cut beef thinly across the grain. Standing time is important for beef, which is best cooked slowly and then allowed to stand. Fast cooking toughens the meat.

Use tenderloin or fillet when cooking beef lightly with vegetable, and rump steak chuck for braising. If the flavor of beef is too strong for you, add a slice of ginger and a few drops of Chinese wine, both of which are excellent taste enhancers.

Chinese Beef Steak *73*
Claypot Beef Stew *73*
Skewered Beef Balls *75*
Sour Apple Beef *75*
Spicy Braised Beef *76*

Chinese Beef Steak

Serves 4
Cooking time: 9½ mins
Preparation: 15 mins
K cal: 260/serve

Ingredients

4 pieces beef steak, each
    120 g (4½ oz) and 2 cm
    (¾ in) thick

A
2 teaspoons wine
1 teaspoon ginger juice
2½ teaspoons light soy
    sauce
1 teaspoon sugar
¼ teaspoon baking soda
dash of pepper

B
1 tablespoon oyster sauce
1 teaspoon sugar
¼ cup water
100 g (3½ oz) onion, sliced thinly
dash of pepper

1½ tablespoons oil

Preparation

Marinate steaks in combined ingredients A for 1 hour. Mix together ingredients B.

Cooking

Preheat a BROWNING DISH on power HIGH for 8 minutes.

Pour in oil and brown seasoned steaks by pressing them with a wooden spatula. Turn steaks over and do the same for the other side.

Pour in ingredients B, then cover and microwave on power HIGH for 1½ minutes.

Claypot Beef Stew

Serves 6
Cooking time: 48 mins
Preparation: 15 mins
K cal: 140/serve

Ingredients
A
300 g (10 oz) beef, tender
    cut
100 g (3½ oz) Chinese
    radish
100 g (3½ oz) carrot
1 cup water

B
3 teaspoons preserved
    soybean paste
1 star anise
4 cloves
1½ teaspoons chopped
    garlic
2 tablespoons oil

Garnish
spring onion and Chinese parsley cut into 2 cm (1 in) lengths

Dip
pineapple chili sauce

Preparation

Slice beef ½ cm (¼ in) thick. Cut Chinese radish and carrot into 2 cm (1 in) wedges.

Cooking

Combine ingredients B in a 3 liter (3 qt) claypot and microwave on power HIGH for 4 minutes, uncovered.

Add ingredients A, cover and microwave on power HIGH for 4 minutes. Then, leaving cover on, microwave on power MEDIUM-LOW for 40 minutes.

Garnish with spring onion and Chinese parsley and serve with the pineapple chili sauce.

Sour Apple Beef (p. 75), Spicy Braised Beef (p. 76)

Skewered Beef Balls

Serves 6
Cooking time: 11 mins
Preparation: 20 mins
K cal: 145/serve

Ingredients
A
250 g (9 oz) beef
1½ teaspoons cornstarch
1 teaspoon ginger juice
1 teaspoon salt
¼ teaspoon baking soda

80 g (3 oz) green pepper
80 g (3 oz) red pepper
80 g (3 oz) onion
10 button mushrooms

10 thin bamboo skewers
2 tablespoons oil

Gravy
1 teaspoon HP sauce
1 teaspoon Worcestershire sauce
2½ teaspoons sugar
1 teaspoon wine
¼ cup water
1 tablespoon tomato sauce

Preparation

Mince ingredients A into a paste and divide into 10 portions. Roll each portion into balls.

Remove seeds from green and red peppers and cut into 10 pieces. Cut onion into wedges and divide into 10 portions.

Pierce a beef ball, a piece each of green and red peppers, a button mushroom and an onion wedge through a thin bamboo skewer.

Cooking

Preheat a BROWNING DISH on power HIGH for 8 minutes.

Pour in oil and place the skewered beef balls and vegetables to brown. After 1 minute, turn over the skewered beef balls and vegetables to brown the other side for another minute.

Pour in gravy mixture, cover and microwave on power HIGH for 3 minutes.

Sour Apple Beef

(photo page 74)

Serves 6
Cooking time: 6½ mins
Standing time: 10 mins
Preparation: 15 mins
K cal: 95/serve

Ingredients
2 green sour apples
150 g (5 oz) beef fillet

A
⅛ teaspoon baking soda
½ teaspoon light soy sauce
½ teaspoon sugar
½ teaspoon wine

B
1 teaspoon chopped garlic
1½ tablespoons oil
1 teaspoon salt
½ teaspoon sugar

Preparation

Wash, core and slice apples. Slice fillet thinly and season with combined ingredients A.

Cooking

Combine ingredients B in a 2 liter (2 qt) shallow casserole and microwave on power HIGH for 3 minutes, uncovered.

Stir in the remaining ingredients, then cover and microwave on power HIGH for 3½ minutes.

Let the Sour Apple Beef STAND for 10 minutes before serving.

NOTE: *Sour apples give a special tangy flavor to beef.*

Spicy Braised Beef

Serves 6
Cooking time: 32 mins
Standing time: 10 mins
Preparation: 15 mins
K cal: 125/serve

Ingredients
300 g (10 oz) beef, tender
 cut
2 teaspoons cornstarch
1½ tablespoons water

A
1 teaspoon Szechuan
 peppercorns, crushed
1 teaspoon black pepper-
 corns, crushed
4 cm (1½ in) cinnamon
 stick
½ tablespoon chopped
 onion
1½ tablespoons oil

B
1 cup water
1½ tablespoons oyster
 sauce
1 teaspoon wine
1 teaspoon brown sugar

Preparation

Slice beef into ½ cm (¼ in) thick slices. Mix cornstarch with 1½ tablespoons water.

Cooking

Combine ingredients A in a 3 liter (3 qt) casserole and microwave on power HIGH for 3 minutes, uncovered.

Add beef slices and combined ingredients B, cover and microwave on power HIGH for 4 minutes. Then, still covered, microwave on power MEDIUM–LOW for 25 minutes.

Immediately after the cooking cycle, stir in cornstarch mixture, cover and let STAND for 10 minutes.

MUTTON

This too is not a favorite meat of the Chinese, because of its distinctly strong flavor. Many rules, therefore, surround the buying and cooking of this meat, some of which are:
- mutton fat should be white but not brittle, brittleness being indicative of age,
- an unduly yellow tinge to mutton fat is accompanied by an unwelcome 'muttony' flavor,
- all fat should be trimmed off, and
- spices or ginger are often added to remove the rank flavor and spices are mainly star anise, cloves, aniseed and cinnamon.

Claypot Mutton (p. 79), Sautéed Chives with Seafood (p. 138)

Claypot Mutton

(photo page 78)

Serves 4
Cooking time: 39 mins
Standing time: 10 mins
Preparation: 10 mins
K cal: 165/serve

Ingredients
300 g (10 oz) mutton
15 g (½ oz) pak kei
10 g (⅓ oz) tong kwai
2 tablespoons wine
1½ cups water
1 teaspoon salt

Preparation

Cut mutton into 2 cm (¾ in) cubes. Lightly wash *pak kei* and *tong kwai*.

Cooking

Combine all ingredients except salt in a 3 liter (3 qt) casserole and microwave on power HIGH for 4 minutes, uncovered. Then cover and simmer on power MEDIUM-LOW for 35 minutes.

Stir in salt, cover and let the pot STAND for 10 minutes, still covered.

NOTE: *This is a particularly bracing combination of ingredients that is ideal during cold weather.*

Ginger Mutton Stew

Serves 4
Cooking time: 42½ mins
Standing time: 10 mins
Preparation: 15 mins
K cal: 200/serve

Ingredients
300 g (10 oz) mutton

A
**½ tablespoon preserved
    soybean paste**
1 teaspoon chopped garlic
½ tablespoon oil
**40 g (1½ oz) ginger, peeled
    and sliced thinly**
**1 teaspoon peppercorns,
    crushed**
2 star anise
5 cloves

B
2 teaspoons cornstarch
1 tablespoon water

1 cup water
½ teaspoon salt
½ teaspoon sugar

Preparation

Cut mutton into 2 cm (¾ in) cubes. Mix ingredients B.

Cooking

Combine ingredients A in a 24 cm (9 in) casserole and microwave on power HIGH for 2½ minutes, uncovered.

Add mutton cubes, water, salt and sugar, then cover and microwave on power HIGH for 5 minutes.

Simmer on power MEDIUM-LOW for 35 minutes, still covered.

Immediately after the cooking cycle, stir in cornstarch mixture, cover and let the casserole STAND for 10 minutes before serving.

CHICKEN

The Chinese have great faith in the healing properties of the fowl: for them black chicken is a tonic for mind, body and sexual vigor, while chicken steamed with rice wine and sesame oil restores strength. What sufferer of a depressing cold does not believe in the therapeutic effects of chicken soup?

This versatile food must be cooked just right to retain its essential sweetness and succulence. When cooking in traditionally stir-fried dishes, use the white breast meat. Cut against the grain, at a slant to get as much flat surface as possible, then marinate in a little baking soda to give it a crunchy texture.

Remove fat and skin before cooking in soups. To keep a whole steamed chicken moist and smooth, plunge it in ice-cold water immediately after steaming.

Shield wings, bone ends, breastbone and backbone with foil (dull surface out) before cooking a whole chicken in the microwave oven. If cooking uneven portions such as drumsticks, cook with the narrower ends in the center of the dish.

Wheel of Fortune (p. 94), Broccoli Special (p. 127)

Deboning Chicken

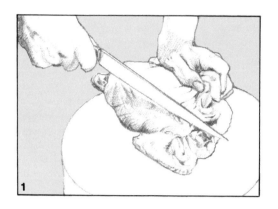

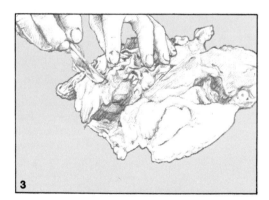

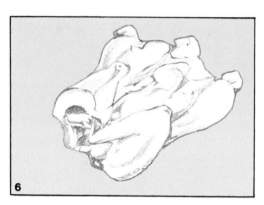

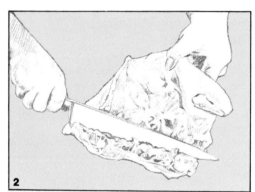

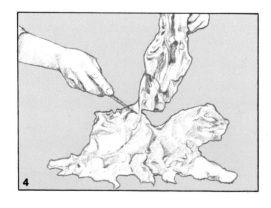

1 Slit chicken breast down the length.

2 With a very sharp knife, separate the meat as close to the bone as possible, on either side of the slit. Lift meat from the rib cage on each side.

3 Cut off breast bone at the joints.

4 You need to remove the whole bone from the neck, using both knife and fingers to push the flesh from the main bone as you progress downward. Cut off at the thigh joints and the whole piece can now be lifted. Keep bones for stock.

5 Separate flesh from the thigh bone with a knife, up to the middle joint. Leave the bone at the end, to give chicken its shape.

6 Leave the wings behind, tucking them neatly into the cavity.

Beggar Chicken

Serves 10
Cooking time: 1 hr
Standing time: 15 mins
Preparation: 10 mins
K cal: 175/serve

Ingredients
1 chicken, 1½ kg (3 lb 5 oz)
10 g (⅓ oz) ginseng (*tong sum*)
10 g (⅓ oz) *tong kwai*
8 g (¼ oz) *pak kei*
5 g (⅕ oz) *kei chee*
5 g (⅕ oz) ginseng (*pow sum*)
10 g (⅓ oz) longan meat
small piece dried Mandarin orange peel
2 cups hot water
1½ teaspoons salt
3 tablespoons Chinese wine

Preparation

Wash the chicken. Combine all ingredients except Chinese wine.

Fill cavity of the chicken with combined ingredients and secure opening with toothpicks.

Cooking

Place stuffed chicken, breast side down, in a 2 liter (2 qt) shallow casserole. Cover with cling wrap and microwave on power MEDIUM-LOW for 1 hour.

Immediately after the cooking cycle, spoon wine over the chicken. Wrap the whole casserole with aluminium foil and let it STAND for 15 minutes before serving.

Boneless Stuffed Chicken

Serves 10
Cooking time: 32 mins
Preparation: 30 mins
K cal: 290/serve

Ingredients
1 chicken, 1⅓ kg (3 lb)
2 teaspoons light soy sauce
1 teaspoon wine
1 teaspoon honey

A
100 g (3½ oz) carrot
10 dried black mushrooms
30 gingko nuts (*pak kor*)
100 g (3½ oz) green peas
1 tablespoon oyster sauce
¼ cup water

1½ teaspoons chopped garlic
1 tablespoon oil
200 g (7 oz) cooked lotus seeds
1 cup cooked rice

Preparation

Clean and debone chicken. Season with soy sauce, wine and honey.

Dice carrot. Soak dried black mushrooms in water to soften, then drain and dice.

Remove shell and skin of gingko nuts. Halve and remove bitter embryo in the center.

Cooking

Combine chopped garlic with oil in a 22 cm (9 in) casserole and microwave on power HIGH for 3 minutes, uncovered.

Add ingredients A and microwave on power HIGH for 4 minutes.

Mix the just-cooked ingredients with cooked lotus seeds and rice to make up the stuffing.

Stuff the boneless chicken with the cooked ingredients and secure opening with toothpicks.

Raise stuffed chicken, breast side up, on a rack in a 4 liter (4 qt) casserole. Microwave on power MEDIUM for 25 minutes.

Cooking is uncovered throughout.

NOTE: *This dish normally takes 1 hour to cook in the conventional way.*

Claypot Chicken Wings

Serves 6
Cooking time: 11½ mins
Standing time: 5 mins
Preparation: 15 mins
K cal: 75/serve

Ingredients
7 chicken wings, 300 g (10 oz)
150 g (5 oz) kale stems
50 g (2 oz) carrot

A
80 g (3 oz) young ginger, chopped finely
10 g (⅓ oz) garlic, chopped finely
1½ tablespoons oil

B
1½ teaspoons wine
1 tablespoon oyster sauce
1 teaspoon cornstarch
¼ cup chicken stock

Preparation

Wash chicken wings. Holding knife at an angle to the stem, cut kale stems into 3 cm (1 in) lengths, about ½ cm (¼ in) thick. Slice carrot thinly.

Cooking

Combine ingredients A in a 2 liter (2 qt) claypot and microwave on power HIGH for 4 minutes, uncovered.

Add chicken wings and combined ingredients B. Cover and microwave on power HIGH for 6 minutes.

Add carrot slices and kale stems. Cover and microwave on power HIGH for 1½ minutes.

Let the claypot STAND for 5 minutes before serving.

Claypot Wine Chicken

Serves 6
Cooking time: 14 mins
Preparation: 5 mins
K cal: 190/serve

Ingredients
A
1 tablespoon chopped garlic
100 g (3½ oz) young ginger, shredded
½ tablespoon sesame oil

600 g (1 lb 5 oz) chicken pieces
1½ teaspoons oyster sauce
3 cups water
4 tablespoons wine

Cooking

Combine ingredients A in a 4 liter (4 qt) claypot and microwave on power HIGH for 4 minutes, uncovered.

Add chicken pieces, oyster sauce and water. Cover and microwave on power HIGH for 10 minutes.

Sprinkle wine over chicken and serve.

Cold Chicken Towers (p. 86), Sesame Seed Chicken (p. 91)

Cold Chicken Towers

(photo page 85)

Serves 6
Cooking time: 6½ mins
Preparation: 15 mins
K cal: 100/serve

Ingredients
200 g (7 oz) chicken breast
150 g (5 oz) shrimp

A
30 g (1 oz) dried black
   mushrooms
½ teaspoon light soy sauce
1 tablespoon water

B
10 g (⅓ oz) gelatin
1¼ cups chicken stock
1 teaspoon wine
1 teaspoon salt
½ teaspoon sugar

100 g (3½ oz) green peas

Garnish
shredded lettuce

12 dariole molds or small
   plastic tumblers

Preparation

Wash chicken breast and leave whole. Shell and devein shrimp.

Soak dried black mushrooms in water and when softened, slice thinly.

Grease the inside of dariole molds or plastic tumblers.

Cooking

Place chicken meat and shrimp on a dinner plate and cover with cling wrap. Microwave on power HIGH for 3 minutes.

Shred cooked chicken and slice the shrimp in half lengthwise.

Combine ingredients A in a small casserole. Cover and microwave on power HIGH for 1½ minutes. Set aside the mushrooms.

Combine ingredients B in a small casserole. Microwave on power HIGH for 2½ minutes, uncovered. Stir halfway through the cooking cycle. Set aside the gelatin mixture.

Assembly

Into each greased mold, put in sliced shrimp, green peas, shredded chicken and sliced mushroom. Top with more shredded chicken. Pour in warm gelatin mixture between layers of ingredients.

Refrigerate to set.

Just before serving, turn molds onto a serving plate and allow Cold Chicken Towers to slide out of the molds. Serve on a bed of shredded lettuce.

NOTE: *A good cold starter for parties, Cold Chicken Towers are ideally served with Thousand Island salad dressing.*

Drunken Chicken

Serves 10
Cooking time: 30 mins
Standing time: 15 mins
Preparation: 10 mins
K cal: 180/serve

Ingredients
1 chicken, 1⅓ kg (3 lb)
150 g (5 oz) coarse salt
2 liters (2 qt) water
200 g (7 oz) ginger
1 teaspoon sesame oil
1 teaspoon sugar
½ cup wine

Preparation

Wash chicken. Mix salt with water and soak the chicken in the salt solution for 3 hours. Mince ginger.

Cut open chicken at breast, spread out and season with minced ginger, sesame oil, sugar and half the wine. Let chicken stand in seasoning for 2 hours.

Cooking

Place seasoned chicken into a 2 liter (2 qt) oval casserole, cover with cling wrap and microwave on power MEDIUM for 30 minutes.

Pour remaining wine over the cooked chicken and let it STAND for 15 minutes, covered, before serving.

NOTE: *This recipe is ideal for women after childbirth. Ginger warms the stomach and wine is excellent for blood circulation.*

Fiery Chicken Cubes

(photo page 104)

Serves 6
Cooking time: 9 mins
Preparation: 15 mins
K cal: 100/serve

Ingredients
300 g (10 oz) chicken breast
¼ teaspoon baking soda

A
15 dried chiles
1 teaspoon chopped ginger
1 teaspoon chopped garlic
1 tablespoon oil

B
100 g (3½ oz) onion
1½ teaspoons hot bean
    sauce
½ teaspoon oyster sauce
1½ teaspoons sugar
1 teaspoon wine

Garnish
chopped spring onion and
    Chinese parsley

Preparation

Cut chicken breast meat into cubes and season with baking soda.

Halve dried chiles and cut onion into wedges.

Cooking

Combine ingredients A in a 24 cm (9 in) shallow casserole and microwave on power HIGH for 4 minutes, uncovered.

Add ingredients B and microwave on power HIGH for 1½ minutes.

Add seasoned chicken cubes and microwave on power MEDIUM for 3½ minutes.

Garnish with chopped spring onion and Chinese parsley and serve.

The casserole remains uncovered throughout cooking.

NOTE: *Dried chiles, common in Indian curries, are also used in Chinese cooking, where they impart a spicy fragrance.*

Gingko Nut Chicken

Serves 6
Cooking time: 20 mins
Preparation: 10 mins
K cal: 210/serve

Ingredients
500 g (1 lb 1 oz) chicken
    pieces
1½ teaspoons cornstarch
½ tablespoon water

A
2 teaspoons ginger juice
2 teaspoons light soy sauce
1 teaspoon sugar
½ teaspoon pepper

B
30 gingko nuts (*pak kor*)
6 red dates
120 g (4 oz) water chestnuts
1 teaspoon light soy sauce
½ cup chicken stock

2 tablespoons oil

Preparation

Steamed chicken pieces with ingredients A. Mix cornstarch with ½ tablespoon water.

Discard shell and skin of gingko nuts. Halve nuts and remove bitter embryo in the center.

Halve red dates and remove stone. Skin water chestnuts and slice them.

Cooking

Preheat a BROWNING DISH on power HIGH for 8 minutes.

Add oil and seasoned chicken pieces and microwave on power HIGH for 1½ minutes, uncovered.

Turn chicken pieces over and microwave on power HIGH for 2½ minutes, uncovered.

Add ingredients B, then cover and microwave on power HIGH for 8 minutes.

Immediately after the cooking cycle, stir in the cornstarch mixture.

Ginseng Chicken

Serves 10
Cooking time: 50 mins
Standing time: 10 mins
Preparation: 5 mins
K cal: 155/serve

Ingredients
1 chicken, 1⅓ kg (3 lb)

A
30 g (1 oz) ginseng (*pow
    sum*), washed lightly
1½ teaspoons salt
½ teaspoon sugar
2 cups water

3 tablespoons wine

Cooking

Combine ingredients A in a 20 cm (8 in) casserole and microwave on power HIGH for 5 minutes, uncovered.

Pour cooked ingredients into the chicken cavity and secure opening with toothpicks.

Place stuffed chicken, breast side up, in a 5 liter (5 qt) casserole. Cover wings, neck, tail and a 4 cm (1½ in) strip of the breast with aluminium foil, dull side out, to prevent drying of chicken.

Cover the casserole and microwave on power MEDIUM-LOW for 45 minutes.

Turn the chicken breast side down halfway through the cooking cycle. Cover with aluminium foil, again dull side out. Cover casserole.

At the end of the cooking time, spoon wine over chicken and let it STAND for 10 minutes, covered during that time.

NOTE: *Ginseng invigorates the internal organs and the nervous system.*

Stuffed Chicken Wings (p. 92), Braised Vegetarian Mix (p. 126)

Golden Lilies Chicken

Serves 6
Cooking time: 15 mins
Preparation: 10 mins
K cal: 210/serve

Ingredients
600 g (1 lb 5 oz) chicken
pieces

A
1 tablespoon oyster sauce
1 teaspoon light soy sauce
1 teaspoon wine
2 teaspoons ginger juice

B
30 dried golden lilies
5 dried black mushrooms
5 red dates

½ tablespoon chopped
garlic
1 tablespoon oil

Preparation

Season chicken pieces with combined ingredients A.

Soak dried golden lilies and dried black mushrooms to soften. Slice mushrooms thinly.

Cut red dates in half and discard stone.

Cooking

Combine chopped garlic with oil in a 24 cm (9 in) casserole and microwave on power HIGH for 3½ minutes, uncovered.

Add ingredients B, cover and microwave on power HIGH for 1½ minutes.

Stir in seasoned chicken pieces, cover and microwave on power MEDIUM for 10 minutes.

NOTE: *Golden lilies are known for their unique sweet flavor. These flowers are said to bloom only in the early morning, and then only for a short while.*

Pak Lan Yoke Kai

Serves 10
Cooking time: 13½ mins
Preparation: 10 mins
K cal: 190/serve

Ingredients
1 chicken, 1⅓ kg (3 lb)
200 g (7 oz) kale

A
4 slices ginger
1 stalk spring onion
10 Szechuan peppercorns

Gravy
1 cup chicken stock
2 teaspoons glutinous rice
wine
1 teaspoon ginger juice
2 teaspoons honey
1 teaspoon salt
2 tablespoons cooked oil
1 teaspoon sesame oil

Preparation

Wash the chicken. Wash kale and arrange on a plate. Cover with cling wrap.

Cooking

Microwave kale on power HIGH for 2 minutes.

Stuff ingredients A in the cavity of the chicken and place it breast side up in a 5 liter (5 qt) casserole. Cover and microwave on power HIGH for 9½ minutes.

Combine gravy ingredients in a small casserole and microwave on power HIGH for 2 minutes, uncovered.

Cut cooked chicken into bite-sized pieces and arrange on top of cooked kale. Pour cooked gravy mixture on top and serve immediately.

NOTE: *This is a very famous restaurant recipe.*

Sesame Seed Chicken

(photo page 85)

Serves 6
Cooking time: 11 mins
Preparation: 5 mins
K cal: 275/serve

Ingredients
3 pieces chicken fillet, 400 g (14 oz)
1 egg, beaten
100 g (3½ oz) sesame seeds
2½ tablespoons oil

Seasoning
3 teaspoons sesame oil
½ teaspoon pepper
2 teaspoons ginger juice
½ teaspoon wine
1 teaspoon sugar
1 teaspoon salt
¼ teaspoon baking soda

Preparation

Season chicken fillet with combined seasoning for 1 hour.

Coat each piece of chicken with beaten egg before coating evenly with sesame seeds.

Cooking

Preheat a BROWNING DISH on power HIGH for 7 minutes.

Add oil and chicken fillet. Microwave on power HIGH for 1 minute, uncovered.

Turn over chicken fillet and microwave on power HIGH for 3 minutes, still uncovered.

Stuffed Chicken Skin

Serves 10
Cooking time: 9½ mins
Preparation: 15 mins
K cal: 150/serve

Ingredients
A
400 g (14 oz) shrimp
½ teaspoon sugar
1 teaspoon salt
1 egg white
¼ teaspoons pepper
1 teaspoon wine
¼ teaspoon baking soda

4 square 8 cm (3 in) pieces dried chicken skin
1 cup almond flakes
2½ tablespoons oil

Preparation

Shell and devein shrimp and mince with rest of ingredients A. Divide the paste into 4 portions.

Spread each portion of minced shrimp into each piece of dried chicken skin and top with almond flakes.

Cooking

Preheat a BROWNING DISH on power HIGH for 6 minutes.

Pour in oil and place open-face chicken skin sandwiches skin side down on the browning dish. Microwave on power HIGH for 3½ minutes, uncovered.

When cooked, slice each piece into 5 pieces and serve immediately.

NOTE: *The best way to dry chicken skin is to place fresh chicken skin on a rack and leave it to dry in the refrigerator for a week.*

Stuffed Chicken Wings

(photo page 89)

Serves 6
Cooking time: 13 mins
Preparation: 30 mins
K cal: 200/serve

Ingredients

12 chicken wings, 1 kg (2
   lb 3oz)

A

1 tablespoon oyster sauce
½ teaspoon HP sauce
1 teaspoon Worcestershire
   sauce
1 teaspoon sugar
1 teaspoon ginger juice
1 teaspoon wine

B

50 g (2 oz) carrot
50 g (2 oz) yam bean
3 dried black mushrooms
4 sprigs Chinese parsley

3 tablespoons oil

Preparation

Debone chicken wing in the following way. With kitchen scissors, cut away tendons at the knuckle joint. Push down the skin with meat until the wing tip joint is reached. Give the joint a twist to remove bone.

Season deboned chicken wings with combined seasoning A.

Shred carrot and yam bean. Soak dried black mushrooms to soften, then slice thinly. Cut each sprig of Chinese parsley into 3 pieces.

Combine ingredients B and divide into 12 portions. Stuff a portion into each deboned chicken wing.

Cooking

Preheat a **BROWNING DISH** on power **HIGH** for 8 minutes.

Add oil and the stuffed chicken wings. Microwave on power **HIGH** for 1½ minutes, uncovered.

Turn chicken wings over and microwave on power **HIGH** for 3½ minutes.

NOTE: *This recipe makes an attractive offering at a dinner party.*

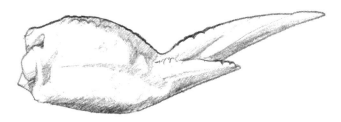

Szechuan Chicken

Serves 6
Cooking time: 8½ mins
Preparation: 10 mins
K cal: 85/serve

Ingredients

250 g (9 oz) chicken breast
1 red chile, chopped
1 teaspoon chopped ginger
1½ tablespoons oil

A
1 teaspoon light soy sauce
1 teaspoon sugar
dash of baking soda

B
80 g (3 oz) Szechuan
    vegetable
6 dried black mushrooms
1 teaspoon hot bean sauce
1 teaspoon light soy sauce
1½ teaspoons sugar
1 teaspoon wine

Preparation

Cut chicken breast meat into strips and season with combined ingredients A.

Wash Szechuan vegetable and cut into strips.

Soak dried black mushrooms in water to soften, then slice thinly.

Cooking

Combine chopped chile, ginger and oil in a 28 cm (11 in) casserole and microwave on power HIGH for 4 minutes, uncovered.

Add ingredients B and microwave on power HIGH for 2 minutes.

Stir in chicken strips and microwave on power HIGH for 2½ minutes.

Leave the casserole uncovered throughout.

Tai Tow Kai

Serves 6
Cooking time: 24 mins
Preparation: 10 mins
K cal: 210/serve

Ingredients

500 g (1 lb 1 oz) chicken
    pieces
150 g (5 oz) salted radish
2 pieces wood ear fungus
    (m*ook yee*), soaked
10 red dates
100 g (3½ oz) onion
20 dried golden lilies,
    soaked

Garnish

spring onion cut into 5 cm
    (2 in) lengths

Preparation

Clean chicken pieces. Cut salted radish into strips and soak for 10 minutes.

Cut softened wood ears into strips. Remove stone from red dates. Cut onion into wedges.

Cooking

Combine all ingredients except the garnish in a 3 liter (3 qt) casserole. Cover and microwave on power HIGH for 4 minutes.

Simmer on power LOW for 20 minutes, still covered. Garnish before serving.

NOTE: *Do not confuse the large pieces of salted radish with the much smaller preserved radish. Refer to notes at the front of the book.*

Wheel of Fortune

(photo page 81)

Serves 10
Cooking time: 15 mins
Preparation: 30 mins
K cal: 185/serve

Ingredients
1 chicken, 1⅓ kg (3 lb)

A
½ tablespoon oyster sauce
1 teaspoon pepper
1 teaspoon sesame oil
1 teaspoon wine
dash of five-spice powder

B
150 g (5 oz) lotus root
20 g (1 oz) carrot
100 g (3½ oz) onion
10 straw mushrooms

Gravy
1 tablespoon oyster sauce
1 cup chicken stock
½ tablespoon cornstarch

1 tablespoon oil for basting

Garnish
10 quail's eggs, hardboiled
    and peeled

Preparation

Debone chicken and season with ingredients A for 1 hour.

Slice lotus root and carrot thinly. Cut onion into wedges.

Combine ingredients B in a 4 liter (4 qt) oval casserole and add the gravy mixture.

Place the seasoned chicken on top of ingredients B.

Cooking

Microwave on power MEDIUM for 15 minutes, uncovered. Baste with oil every 5 minutes of the cooking cycle.

Surround the chicken with quail's eggs and serve.

NOTE: *Lotus root slices resemble bullock cart wheels and quail's eggs represent fortune, hence 'Wheel of Fortune'.*

Wood Ear Ginger Chicken

Serves 4
Cooking time: 12½ mins
Standing time: 10 mins
Preparation: 10 mins
K cal: 400/serve

Ingredients
300 g (10 oz) chicken breast
    meat
3 pieces wood ear fungus
    (*mook yee*)

A
50 g (1¾ oz) young ginger,
    shredded
1½ teaspoons chopped
    garlic
1½ tablespoons sesame oil

100 g (3½ oz) boiled
    peanuts
1½ teaspoons salt
1 cup water
1 cup glutinous rice wine

Preparation

Remove skin and fat from chicken and slice meat.

Soak wood ears and shred.

Cooking

Combine ingredients A in a 3 liter (3 qt) casserole and microwave on power HIGH for 4½ minutes, uncovered.

Add chicken, wood ears, peanuts, salt and water. Cover and microwave on power HIGH for 8 minutes.

Pour in the glutinous rice wine, cover the casserole and let it STAND for 10 minutes.

NOTE: *This particular Ginger Chicken is usually served during the confinement period. Relatives are invited to share this dish 12 days after the baby is born. Wood ears are said to 'loosen clogged blood'. The Chinese believe that it is particularly important to remove chicken skin and fat when cooking this dish for women who have undergone surgery as these parts would cause stitched wounds to heal 'untidily'.*

Yee Heong Kai

Serves 6
Cooking time: 15 mins
Preparation: 5 mins
K cal: 240/serve

Ingredients
500 g (1 lb 1 oz) chicken
    pieces
⅓ cup cornstarch

A
1 piece fermented beancurd
    (*foo yee*)
1½ teaspoons wine
2 teaspoons sugar
2 teaspoons *hoisin* sauce
½ tablespoon oyster sauce
½ teaspoon pepper

3 tablespoons oil

Preparation

Season chicken pieces with ingredients A for 1 hour before coating with cornstarch.

Cooking

Preheat a BROWNING DISH on power HIGH for 8 minutes.

Add oil and the seasoned chicken pieces. Microwave on power HIGH for 7 minutes, uncovered.

Turn chicken pieces over halfway through the cooking cycle.

Ginger Duck (p. 99), Lilies on Greens (p. 133)

DUCK

Duck makes a good roast because of the thickness of the layer of fat beneath the skin. Remove the gamey odor of duck by squeezing the tip of the rear end (Asians call this the 'bishop's nose') to release the wax.

Roasting in the microwave oven helps preserve the shape and flavor of duck, but it is still advisable to deep-fry the duck for a short period to obtain a crisp, glazed skin.

As for chicken, cover bone tips, wings and breast and back bones with strips of foil (dull surface out). Where necessary, refer also to the deboning notes in the chapter on chicken.

Claypot Duck with Sour Plum Sauce

Serves 6
Cooking time: 33½ mins
Standing time: 10 mins
Preparation: 15 mins
K cal: 100/serve

Ingredients
500 g (1 lb 1 oz) duck pieces
80 g (3 oz) spring onion
1½ teaspoons cornstarch
1 tablespoon water

A
20 g (¾ oz) pickled spring garlic
20 g (¾ oz) pickled ginger
1½ teaspoons chopped garlic
2 cm (¾ in) cinnamon stick
1½ tablespoons oil

B
10 g (⅓ oz) sour plums
15 g (½ oz) red chiles
2 teaspoons brown sugar
½ cup water
1½ teaspoons salt

Preparation

Remove skin and fat of duck pieces.

Wash spring onion under running water and cut into 3 cm (1 in) lengths.

Mix cornstarch with 1 tablespoon water. Slice pickled spring garlic and ginger.

Cooking

Combine ingredients A in a 2 liter (2 qt) claypot. Microwave on power HIGH for 3½ minutes, uncovered.

Stir in ingredients B and duck pieces. Cover and microwave on power MEDIUM for 30 minutes.

Immediately after the cooking cycle, stir in the cornstarch mixture and spring onion. Cover and let it STAND for 10 minutes before serving.

Eight Jewel Duck

(photo page 100)

Serves 10
Cooking time: 35 mins
Standing time: 20 mins
Preparation: 30 mins
K cal: 165/serve

Ingredients
1 duck, 1⅘ kg (4 lb)
1 tablespoon oyster sauce

Stuffing
30 gingko nuts (*pak kor*)
100 g (3½ oz) cooked lotus
   seeds
5 dried black mushrooms,
   soaked
80 g (3 oz) carrot
100 g (3½ oz) green peas
100 g (3½ oz) bamboo
   shoot
50 g (2 oz) dried cuttlefish,
   soaked
2 cm (¾ in) cinnamon
   stick
1 star anise
3 cloves
1½ tablespoons oyster
   sauce
4 tablespoons water

oil for basting

Preparation

Debone duck and season with oyster sauce.

Remove shell and skin of gingko nuts. Halve and remove the bitter embryo in the center.

Dice softened mushrooms, carrot, bamboo shoot and cuttlefish.

Combine ingredients for stuffing and stuff into deboned duck. Secure opening with toothpicks.

Cooking

Brush oil all over the stuffed duck and raise it on a rack in a 4 liter (4 qt) casserole. Cover the casserole and microwave on power MEDIUM for 35 minutes.

Baste stuffed duck with oil every 10 minutes of the cooking cycle.

Immediately after the cooking cycle, wrap the whole casserole with aluminium foil and let it STAND for 20 minutes to finish cooking.

NOTE: *The Cantonese name of this dish is Part Poh Ngap.*

Ginger Duck

(photo page 96)

Serves 6
Cooking time: 39 mins
Standing time: 10 mins
Preparation: 5 mins
K cal: 95/serve

Ingredients
600 g (1 lb 5 oz) duck
   pieces
1 tablespoon cornstarch
1½ tablespoons water

A
150 g (5 oz) young ginger,
   sliced
½ tablespoon chopped
   garlic
1 tablespoon chopped
   preserved soy beans
1 tablespoon oil

B
½ tablespoon oyster sauce
2 cups water

Preparation

Wash the duck pieces. Mix cornstarch with 1½ tablespoons water.

Cooking

Combine ingredients A in a 4 liter (4 qt) casserole and microwave on power HIGH for 4 minutes, uncovered.

Add ingredients B and duck pieces. Cover and microwave on power HIGH for 5 minutes.

Simmer on power MEDIUM-LOW for 30 minutes, covered.

Immediately after the cooking cycle, stir in the cornstarch mixture, cover the casserole and let it STAND for 10 minutes.

天柱主中流
月下开菱鏡
雲間結彩樓

Eight Jewel Duck (p. 99), Braised Tientsin Cabbage with Ham (p. 126)

Heong So Ngap

Serves 6
Cooking time: 33 mins
Preparation: 5 mins
K cal: 160/serve

Ingredients
**600 g (1 lb 5 oz) duck
pieces**
1 tablespoon cornstarch
1½ tablespoons water
oil for frying

A
**½ teaspoon five-spice
powder**
2 teaspoons light soy sauce
1 teaspoon sugar

B
**½ teaspoon Szechuan
pepper**
**1 teaspoon black pepper-
corns**
2 teaspoons light soy sauce
¼ teaspoon dark soy sauce
1 star anise
3 cloves
2½ cups water

Preparation

Season duck pieces with ingredients A for 1 hour.

Mix cornstarch with 1½ tablespoons water.

Cooking

In the conventional way, deep-fry seasoned duck pieces in oil for 3 minutes. Drain duck pieces.

Combine deep-fried duck pieces with ingredients B in a 4 liter (4 qt) casserole. Cover casserole and microwave on power HIGH for 5 minutes.

Next, simmer on power MEDIUM-LOW for 25 minutes, covered.

Immediately after the cooking cycle, stir in the cornstarch mixture to thicken the gravy. Serve immediately.

NOTE: *Leftover roast duck can be used in this recipe. Simply skip the first step, the deep-frying of duck pieces.*

Teochew Duck

(photo page 132)

Serves 10
Cooking time: 42 mins
Standing time: 25 mins
Preparation: 10 mins
K cal: 100/serve

Ingredients

1 duck, 1⁴/₅ kg (4 lb)
1 tablespoon cornstarch
1½ tablespoons water

A

1 teaspoon light soy sauce
1 teaspoon dark soy sauce
½ teaspoon sugar

B

60 g (2 oz) ginger, sliced
60 g (2 oz) galangal, sliced
1 star anise
5 cloves
4 cm (1½ in) cinnamon
    stick
2 tablespoons oyster sauce
1½ teaspoons wine
1½ cups water

Preparation

Season duck with combined ingredients A. Mix cornstarch with 1½ tablespoons water.

Cooking

Combine ingredients B in a small casserole. Microwave on power HIGH for 5 minutes, uncovered.

Pour cooked ingredients into the duck cavity and secure opening with cocktail sticks.

Raise duck on a rack in a 4 liter (4 qt) casserole. Cover and microwave on power MEDIUM for 35 minutes.

Immediately after the cooking cycle, wrap the casserole with aluminium foil and let it STAND for 25 minutes to finish cooking.

Remove duck from casserole, cut into bite-size pieces and arrange on a serving plate.

Add cornstarch mixture to the duck drippings left in the casserole and microwave on power HIGH for 2 minutes to make gravy.

Pour gravy over the duck pieces and serve.

NOTE: *This braised duck takes 3½ hours cooked the conventional way, over a slow fire.*

Water Chestnut and Mushroom Duck

Serves 6
Cooking time: 11 mins
Preparation: 15 mins
K cal: 130/serve

Ingredients

300 g (10 oz) duck breast
10 dried black mushrooms,
    soaked
2 pieces wood ear fungus
    (*mook yee*), soaked
10 water chestnuts
¼ cup water

A
1½ teaspoons pepper
1½ tablespoons oil

B
3 teaspoons light soy sauce
1½ teaspoons wine
2 teaspoons sugar
¼ teaspoons pepper

Garnish
spring onion and Chinese
    parsley cut into 4 cm
    (1½ in) lengths

Preparation

Slice duck breast, dried black mushrooms, wood ears and water chestnuts.

Cooking

Combine ingredients A and mushroom slices in a 24 cm (9 in) casserole and microwave on power HIGH for 3½ minutes, uncovered.

Add ingredients B and microwave on power HIGH for 1 minute, uncovered.

Add remaining ingredients except the garnish. Cover and microwave on power HIGH for 6½ minutes.

Garnish and serve.

Spicy Padi Frogs (p. 106), Fiery Chicken Cubes (p. 87)

FROG

The Chinese believe that frogs eaten at regular intervals are excellent for cleansing the blood and aiding a troubled complexion. They are also good for sharp vision. The frog, however, is eaten more as a food delicacy than as a medicinal food. Its flesh is like tender spring chicken.

The paddy frog, the species used in these recipes, is found in paddy fields, marshland and banks of streams. It is caught at night after a heavy shower in the late afternoon.

Check for freshness. Fresh meat is glossy and white. Frozen paddy frogs lose their gloss and whiteness. Each frog is cut into four or six pieces, depending on its size.

Spicy Paddy Frogs

(photo page 104)

Serves 4
Cooking time: 10 mins
Preparation: 15 mins
K cal: 105/serve

Ingredients
300 g (10 oz) paddy frogs

A
20 g (¾ oz) dried chiles
80 g (3 oz) onion
1½ teaspoons chopped garlic
1½ tablespoons oil

B
1 teaspoon hot bean sauce
1 tablespoon oyster sauce
1 teaspoon sugar
1 teaspoon wine

Preparation

Wash paddy frogs and cut into pieces.

Wash and cut dried chiles into 3 cm (1 in) lengths. Cut onion into wedges.

Cooking

Combine ingredients A in a 3 liter (3 qt) shallow casserole. Cover and microwave on power HIGH for 4 minutes.

Add combined ingredients B and microwave on power HIGH for 1½ minutes, uncovered.

Add paddy frogs. Cover the casserole and microwave on power HIGH for 4½ minutes. Stir after 2½ minutes of the cooking cycle.

Spring Frogs

Serves 4
Cooking time: 9 mins
Standing time: 5 mins
Preparation: 15 mins
K cal: 100/serve

Ingredients
300 g (10 oz) paddy frogs
80 g (3 oz) spring onion

A
80 g (3 oz) young ginger, sliced
1½ teaspoons chopped garlic
1½ tablespoons oil

B
1 tablespoon oyster sauce
1 teaspoon sugar
1 teaspoon wine

Preparation

Wash paddy frogs and cut into pieces. Cut spring onion into 2 cm (¾ in) lengths.

Cooking

Combine ingredients A in a 24 cm (9 in) casserole and microwave on power HIGH for 3½ minutes, uncovered.

Stir in ingredients B and microwave on power HIGH for 1 minute, uncovered.

Add paddy frogs, cover and microwave on power HIGH for 4½ minutes.

Immediately after the cooking cycle, add spring onion, cover and let casserole STAND for 5 minutes before serving.

Steamed Paddy Frogs

Serves 4
Cooking time: 4 mins
Standing time: 5 mins
Preparation: 10 mins
K cal: 35/serve

Ingredients
300 g (10 oz) paddy frogs

A
3 teaspoons wine
2½ teaspoons ginger juice
1 tablespoon light soy sauce
1 teaspoon sugar
3 tablespoons water

Garnish
chopped spring onion and
Chinese parsley

Preparation

Clean paddy frogs and cut into pieces. Place frog pieces in a 24 cm (9 in) casserole.

Cooking

Pour combined ingredients A over the paddy frogs. Cover the casserole and microwave on power HIGH for 4 minutes.

Let the casserole STAND for 5 minutes before serving, garnished with chopped spring onion and Chinese parsley.

NOTE: *Paddy frogs are politely called teen kai in Cantonese - paddy chicken. They do taste like young spring chicken! Actually, paddy frogs are no mere delicacy: they are believed to be good for babies who suffer skin roughness and rashes.*

BEANCURD

Soybean products appear frequently in Chinese cooking. Recipes in which beancurd is present as a main ingredient are given below, but in fact beancurd is present in many other recipes in this book, in one form or another. A glance at the list of beancurd products in the notes on ingredients at the beginning of the book will indicate the range in existence for Chinese cooking.

The blandness of beancurd and its vast range of textures from elasticity to velvety softness make it an excellent ingredient for many vegetarian and meat recipes. Beancurd sheets, for example, cunningly wrapped around a thin stick of sugarcane, pass for 'chicken drumstick'. On a hot afternoon, a cool soft beancurd square, topped with chopped spring onion and chiles, crispy minced garlic, and soy sauce dribbling down its sides makes a perfect one-dish meal.

Soft beancurd, annoyingly breakable in stir-fried recipes or while being transferred into a serving bowl, retains its shape when cooked in its serving plate or casserole in the microwave oven.

Stuffed Beancurd (p. 115), Snow Peas with Beef (p. 139)

Beancurd Pork

Serves 6
Cooking time: 9 mins
Preparation: 15 mins
K cal: 230/serve

Ingredients
300 g (10 oz) firm yellow
  beancurd squares (*tau
  yoon*)
150 g (5 oz) belly pork
½ cup water

A
1½ teaspoons preserved soy
  beans
2 red chiles
15 g (½ oz) garlic
1 tablespoon oil

Preparation

Slice beancurd into ½ cm (¼ in) thickness. Slice belly pork thinly.

Mince ingredients A to a paste.

Cooking

Place ingredients A in a 24 cm (9 oz) casserole and microwave on power HIGH for 4 minutes, uncovered.

Add remaining ingredients, then cover and microwave on power HIGH for 5 minutes.

Beancurd with Egg Sauce

(photo page 29)

Serves 4
Cooking time: 10 mins
Preparation: 10 mins
K cal: 195/serve

Ingredients
300 g (10 oz) soft white
  beancurd squares (*suey
  tau foo*)
2 tablespoons oil
1 egg, beaten

A
1 cup chicken stock
1 teaspoon wine
1 teaspoon salt
2 teaspoons cornstarch

B
100 g (3½ oz) shrimp,
  chopped
100 g (3½ oz) crabmeat

Garnish
chopped spring onion and
  Chinese parsley

Cooking

Combine ingredients A in a 15 cm (6 in) casserole and microwave on power HIGH for 2½ minutes, uncovered.

Add ingredients B and microwave on power HIGH for 1½ minutes, still uncovered. Set aside this gravy mixture.

Preheat a BROWNING DISH on power HIGH for 5 minutes. Pour in oil and beancurd. After 1 minute, turn the beancurd over. Pour in the cooked gravy and beaten egg. Cover and microwave on power HIGH for 1 minute.

Sprinkle with chopped spring onion and Chinese parsley and serve.

Braised Beancurd with Saltfish

Serves 6
Cooking time: 14 mins
Standing time: 10 mins
Preparation: 10 mins
K cal: 180/serve

Ingredients
**200 g (7 oz) firm white
beancurd squares (*tau
foo*)**

A
150 g (5 oz) belly pork
50 g (1³/₄ oz) ginger
2 red chiles

B
100 g (3¹/₂ oz) saltfish
1 teaspoon wine
1¹/₂ teaspoons sugar
1 cup water

Preparation

Wash and slice firm beancurd into ¹/₂ cm (¹/₄ in) thick pieccs.

Slice belly pork and saltfish to ¹/₂ cm (¹/₄ in) thickness. Slice ginger and red chiles thinly.

Cooking

Combine ingredients A in a 3 liter (5 pt) casserole and microwave on power HIGH for 4 minutes, uncovered.

Add ingredients B, then cover and microwave on power MEDIUM for 10 minutes.

Add the beancurd, cover and let it STAND for 10 minutes before serving.

Steamed Beancurd with Dried Shrimps (p. 115), Stuffed Hairy Marrow (p. 144)

Claypot Beancurd

Serves 6
Cooking time: 9½ mins
Standing time: 10 mins
Preparation: 10 mins
K cal: 70/serve

Ingredients

A
2 teaspoons chopped shallot
1 teaspoon chopped garlic
1 tablespoon oil

B
30 g (1 oz) carrot, sliced
    thinly
2 dried black mushrooms,
    soaked to soften and
    sliced thinly
10 button mushrooms

C
1 cup chicken stock
1 tablespoon oyster sauce
2 teaspoons cornstarch

100 g (3½ oz) deep-fried
    soft beancurd squares
    (*chow suey tau foo*)
80 g (3 oz) snow peas

Cooking

Combine ingredients A in a 3 liter (3 qt) claypot and microwave on power HIGH for 4 minutes, uncovered.

Add ingredients B and C.

Cover and microwave on power HIGH for 5½ minutes. After 3 minutes of the cooking cycle, stir and add beancurd, then finish cooking cycle.

Add snow peas, cover and let the claypot STAND for 10 minutes before serving.

Hot Plate Beancurd

Serves 6
Cooking time: 11½ mins
Standing time: 5 mins
Preparation: 15 mins
K cal: 155/serve

Ingredients
350 g (12 oz) soft white
    beancurd squares (*suey
    tau foo*)

A
2 dried black mushrooms
100 g (3½ oz) lean pork
100 g (3½ oz) shrimp
1 cup chicken stock
1 tablespoon oyster sauce
1½ teaspoons cornstarch

1½ teaspoons chopped
    shallots
1½ tablespoons oil

Garnish
chopped spring onion

Preparation

Wash beancurd and set it aside.

Soak dried black mushrooms in water to soften. Chop mushrooms, pork and shrimp.

Cooking

Combine chopped shallots with 1 tablespoon oil in a 24 cm (9 in) casserole and microwave on power HIGH for 3 minutes, uncovered.

Add ingredients A, then cover and microwave on power HIGH for 3½ minutes. Set cooked gravy aside.

Preheat a BROWNING DISH on power HIGH for 5 minutes. Pour in remaining ½ tablespoon oil, place beancurd on oil and allow it to sizzle.

Pour cooked gravy mixture over the beancurd, cover the casserole and let it STAND for 5 minutes.

Garnish with chopped spring onion and serve.

Mah Poh Tau Foo

Serves 6
Cooking time: 7½ mins
Preparation: 15 mins
K cal: 150/serve

Ingredients
300 g (10 oz) soft white
  beancurd squares (*suey
  tau foo*)

A
50 g (1½ oz) Szechuan
  vegetables
1½ teaspoons hot bean
  sauce
1½ teaspoons chopped
  shallot
1½ tablespoons oil

B
100 g (3½ oz) minced lean
  pork
4 dried black mushrooms
50 g (2 oz) carrot
¼ cup water
1 teaspoon sugar

Preparation

Wash beancurd and set aside. Chop Szechuan vegetable.

Soak dried black mushrooms to soften them before chopping with the carrot.

Cooking

Combine ingredients A in a 24 cm (9 in) casserole and microwave on power HIGH for 4 minutes, uncovered.

Add ingredients B and microwave on power HIGH for 2½ minutes, still uncovered.

Add the beancurd, then cover and microwave on power HIGH for 1 minute.

Scrambled Beancurd with Fish Paste

Serves 6
Cooking time: 5½ mins
Preparation: 10 mins
K cal: 90/serve

Ingredients
200 g (7 oz) soft white
  beancurd squares (*suey
  tau foo*)
150 g (5 oz) fish paste
1½ teaspoons light soy
  sauce
1 tablespoon cooked oil
50 g (1½ oz) soft-textured
  saltfish (*moi heong*)

Garnish
chopped spring onion

Preparation

Wash beancurd. Mash with fish paste in a shallow 1 liter (1 qt) casserole. Add light soy sauce and cooked oil.

Slice saltfish thin.

Cooking

Place sliced saltfish between paper towels and toast it by microwaving on power HIGH for 1½ minutes. Chop finely.

Sprinkle toasted saltfish on top of the beancurd mixture. Cover and microwave on power MEDIUM for 4 minutes.

Garnish with chopped spring onion and serve.

NOTE: *Lo Siew Ping Onn is the Cantonese name for this recipe. Lo siew means 'old folk' and ping onn means 'peace and tranquility'. This dish is thus named because of its nutritious and easily digestible nature to the older generation.*

Steamed Beancurd with Dried Shrimp

(photo page 112)

Serves 6
Cooking time: 7½ mins
Preparation: 10 mins
K cal: 140/serve

Ingredients
400 g (14 oz) soft white
    beancurd squares (*suey*
    tau foo)
40 g (1½ oz) dried shrimp
30 g (1 oz) shallots
1 tablespoon oyster sauce
1 tablespoon hot water
3 tablespoons oil

Garnish
15 g (½ oz) spring onion,
    chopped finely

Preparation

Place soft beancurd, whole, on a 30 cm (12 in) plate. Wash and chop dried shrimp. Slice shallots thinly. Mix oyster sauce with hot water.

Cooking

Toast dried shrimp: place them in a plate and microwave on power HIGH for 2½ minutes, stirring every minute.

Combine sliced shallots and oil in a small bowl and microwave on power HIGH for 3½ minutes. Set aside.

Microwave beancurd on its plate on power HIGH for 1½ minutes.

Immediately after the cooking cycle, dribble oyster sauce mixture over beancurd, sprinkle with cooked shallots and oil, then with toasted dried shrimp. Garnish with chopped spring onion.

Stuffed Beancurd

(photo page 109)

Serves 10
Cooking time: 3½ mins
Preparation: 15 mins
K cal: 35/serve

Ingredients
12 pieces deep-fried
    beancurd squares (*tau*
    foo pok)
80 g (3 oz) beansprouts
80 g (3 oz) cucumber
80 g (3 oz) yam bean

Dip
pineapple chili sauce

Preparation

Cut each deep-fried beancurd square into 2 triangles and make a deep slit in the cut side.

Pluck off 'tails' of beansprouts and wash. Shred cucumber and yam bean.

Cooking

Place deep-fried beancurd triangles between paper towels and microwave on power HIGH for 2½ minutes to crisp them.

Place beansprouts on a dinner plate, cover with cling wrap and microwave on power HIGH for 1 minute.

Stuff crisp beancurd triangles with beansprouts, shredded cucumber and yam bean.

Serve with a pineapple chili sauce dip.

NOTE: *Stuffed Beancurd is ideal for buffet parties.*

Stir-fried Leek (p. 143), Claypot Spicy Spare Ribs (p. 65)

VEGETABLES

It is a well known fact that all vegetables are more nutritious and flavorful when cooked in the microwave oven. They also retain their texture. Only a few spoonfuls of water are required to create steam to cook the vegetables. A few tips on cooking the various kinds:

- cover all vegetables with plastic wrap, as they tend to dry up,
- vegetables with a high water content such as leafy vegetables and beansprouts do not require any water to cook - simply wash and cook while still wet,
- use a wide container and spread the vegetables rather than piling them in many layers,
- cut gourds and roots such as angled loofah and carrot into equal-sized pieces so they cook evenly,
- peel off the fibrous tough stem surface of some leafy vegetables such as kale, as it prolongs cooking time, and
- cook stems first, adding leaves only when stems have begun to change color, or leaves will disintegrate while stems are still cooking.

Vegetables may provide vitamin and roughage to modern nutritionists, but the Chinese know they may do more. Leafy vegetables aggravate the 'wind' problem inside the bodies of women after childbirth and should be avoided at all cost. Only dried *mooi choy* is allowed. Celery tea helps lower blood pressure, and to this end celery is boiled till it yellows and the liquid strained and drunk; a fresh lot is brewed on alternate days. Cabbage stimulates the body's plumbing, while white Chinese radish relieves a hangover. Garlic kills germs and tones the blood and water chestnuts sharpen sight and hearing. And these are only some of the more commonly known home cures!

As one has a choice of meat for any meal, but at least one vegetable must appear at every meal, we offer a greater selection in this chapter than in any other.

Angled Loofah

Serves 6
Cooking time: 8½ mins
Preparation: 15 mins
K cal: 75/serve

Ingredients
250 g (9 oz) angled loofah
150 g (5 oz) cuttlefish
5 g (⅕ oz) cloud ear fungus
  (*wan yee*)

A
100 g (3½ oz) onions
1½ tablespoons oil

1 tablespoon oyster sauce
¼ cup water

Preparation

Peel off tough skin of angled loofah and cut into wedges. Clean cuttlefish and cut into bite-sized pieces.

Soak cloud ears to soften, then drain off water. Cut onions into wedges.

Cooking

Combine ingredients A in a 4 liter (4 qt) casserole. Microwave on power HIGH for 2½ minutes, uncovered.

Add remaining ingredients except cloud ears. Cover and microwave on power HIGH for 4½ minutes.

Stir in cloud ears, cover and microwave on power HIGH for 1½ minutes.

Arrowhead with Shredded Pork

Serves 6
Cooking time: 14 mins
Preparation: 15 mins
K cal: 190/serve

Ingredients
250 g (9 oz) arrowhead

A
150 g (5 oz) belly pork
1 piece red fermented
  beancurd (*nam yee*)
1 teaspoon chopped garlic
1½ tablespoons oil

1 teaspoon wine
1 cup water

Preparation

Tear off loose skin of arrowhead and crush them with the flat side of a chopper.

Cut belly pork into strips.

Cooking

Combine ingredients A in a 3 liter (3 qt) casserole and microwave on power HIGH for 4 minutes, uncovered.

Add the remaining ingredients. Cover and microwave on power MEDIUM for 10 minutes.

Arrowhead with Waxed Duck

Serves 6
Cooking time: 14 mins
Standing time: 10 mins
Preparation: 15 mins
K cal: 210/serve

Ingredients

250 g (9 oz) arrowhead
150 g (5 oz) waxed duck
1½ teaspoons wine
50 g (1½ oz) rock sugar
1 cup water

Preparation

Tear loose skin from arrowhead and crush with the flat side of a chopper.

Wash the waxed duck with boiling water to remove excess oil and cut into bite-sized pieces.

Cooking

Combine all ingredients in a 4 liter (4 qt) casserole. Cover and microwave on power HIGH for 4 minutes, then on power MEDIUM for 10 minutes.

Let the casserole STAND for 10 minutes, covered, before serving.

Cabbage Rolls (p. 127), Sizzling Liver (p. 68)

Beansprout Omelette

Serves 6
Cooking time: 9 mins
Preparation: 10 mins
K cal: 105/serve

Ingredients
100 g (3½ oz) beansprouts

A
100 g (3½ oz) shrimp
2 cloves garlic
1 red chile

2 tablespoons oil
3 eggs, beaten
½ teaspoons salt
1 teaspoon light soy sauce

Preparation

Wash and remove 'tails' of beansprouts.

Shell and devein shrimp, then chop coarsely. Chop garlic and chile coarsely.

Cooking

Combine ingredients A with 1 tablespoon oil in a small casserole. Microwave on power HIGH for 2½ minutes, uncovered.

When cool, stir in the remaining ingredients (except oil).

Preheat a BROWNING DISH on power HIGH for 5 minutes.

Add remaining 1 tablespoon oil and pour in the cooked mixture. Microwave on power HIGH for 1½ minutes, uncovered.

Immediately at the end of the cooking cycle, fold the cooked omelette into an envelope.

Beansprouts with Saltfish

(photo page 70)

Serves 6
Cooking time: 9 mins
Standing time: 5 mins
Preparation: 10 mins
K cal: 70/serve

Ingredients
300 g (10 oz) beansprouts
50 g (1½ oz) chives
80 g (3 oz) saltfish

A
1 red chile, chopped
4 cloves garlic, chopped
1 tablespoon oil

1½ teaspoons light soy
    sauce

Preparation

Wash beansprouts and remove 'tails'. Wash chives under running water and cut to 3 cm (1 in) lengths.

Slice saltfish finely.

Cooking

Sandwich saltfish slices between paper towels and microwave on power HIGH for 4 minutes to crisp. Set aside.

Combine ingredients A in a 24 cm (9 in) shallow casserole and microwave on power HIGH for 3 minutes, uncovered.

Add all the other ingredients. Cover the casserole with cling wrap and microwave on power HIGH for 2 minutes.

Let the casserole STAND for 5 minutes before serving.

Bitter Gourd with Beef

Serves 6
Cooking time: 9 mins
Standing time: 5 mins
Preparation: 10 mins
K cal: 90/serve

Ingredients
300 g (10 oz) bitter gourd
1 teaspoon salt
150 g (5 oz) beef
1/8 teaspoon baking soda

A
1 1/2 teaspoons chopped
    garlic
1 tablespoon chopped
    preserved soy beans
1 teaspoon sugar
1 1/2 tablespoons oil

1/4 cup water
1/2 teaspoon cornstarch

Preparation

Halve the bitter gourd lengthwise and remove seeds. Slice bitter gourd thinly. Sprinkle salt on the slices and wash away the salt after 10 minutes.

Slice beef and marinate with baking soda and cornstarch.

Cooking

Combine ingredients A in a 24 cm (9 in) casserole. Microwave on power HIGH for 3 1/2 minutes, uncovered.

Add bitter gourd and water and stir evenly. Cover and microwave on power HIGH for 3 1/2 minutes.

Stir in beef slices. Cover and microwave on power HIGH for 2 minutes.

Let the casserole STAND for 5 minutes, covered, before serving.

Braised Bitter Gourd with Chicken

Serves 6
Cooking time: 21 mins
Standing time: 10 mins
Preparation: 15 mins
K cal: 190/serve

Ingredients
300 g (10 oz) bitter gourd
1 teaspoon salt
1 1/2 teaspoons cornstarch
1 1/2 tablespoons water
400 g (14 oz) chicken pieces

A
1 tablespoon oyster sauce
1 teaspoon ginger juice
1 teaspoon wine

3 tablespoons oil
3/4 cup chicken stock
2 teaspoons light soy sauce

Preparation

Remove seeds from bitter gourd, cut into 2 x 5 cm (1 x 2 in) sticks and sprinkle salt over the pieces. Wash away salt after 10 minutes.

Mix cornstarch with 1 1/2 tablespoons water.

Marinate chicken pieces with ingredients A.

Cooking

Preheat a BROWNING DISH on power HIGH for 8 minutes.

Add oil and chicken. Microwave on power HIGH for 3 minutes, uncovered. Strain off oil.

Add bitter gourd, chicken stock and soy sauce. Cover and microwave on power MEDIUM for 10 minutes.

Immediately after the cooking cycle, stir in the cornstarch mixture. Cover and let dish STAND for 10 minutes before serving.

Mushroom Medley (p. 134), Szechuan Mixed Vegetables (p. 145)

Braised Hairy Marrow

Serves 6
Cooking time: 13 mins
Preparation: 10 mins
K cal: 35/serve

Ingredients
1 hairy marrow, 150 g (5
   oz)
2 dried scallops
5 red dates
1 cup water
4 sheets dried sweet
   beancurd sheets (*tim
   chook*)
1½ teaspoons cornstarch
1 tablespoon water
1½ teaspoons salt

Preparation

Scrape skin from hairy marrow and cut into 3 cm (1 in) thick slices.

Quarter each scallop. Wash and discard stone of red dates. Soak scallops and red dates in 1 cup water.

Cut each beancurd sheet into quarters. Mix cornstarch with 1 tablespoon water.

Cooking

Combine all ingredients (except cornstarch mixture) in a 5 liter (5 qt) casserole. Cover and microwave on power HIGH for 4 minutes.

Simmer on power MEDIUM-LOW for 8 minutes, covered.

Stir in cornstarch mixture and microwave on power HIGH for 1 minute, uncovered.

Braised Tientsin Cabbage

Serves 10
Cooking time: 9 mins
Preparation: 10 mins
K cal: 60/serve

Ingredients
150 g (5 oz) Tientsin
   cabbage stems
100 g (3½ oz) belly pork
1½ teaspoons cornstarch
1 tablespoon water

A
100 g (3½ oz) carrots
3 dried black mushrooms,
   soaked
10 button mushrooms
10 straw mushrooms
1 cup water
1 tablespoon oyster sauce
1 teaspoon light soy sauce

Preparation

Wash and cut Tientsin cabbage stems into bite-sized pieces. Cut belly pork into strips. Mix cornstarch with 1 tablespoon water.

Slice carrots ½ cm (¼ in) thick. Slice black mushrooms finely.

Cooking

Microwave belly pork strips in a 5 liter (5 qt) casserole on power HIGH for 2 minutes, uncovered.

Add ingredients A, cover and microwave on power HIGH for 6 minutes.

Stir in cornstarch mixture and microwave on power HIGH for 1 minute.

Let the casserole STAND covered for 10 minutes before serving.

Braised Tientsin Cabbage with Ham

(photo page 100)

Serves 6
Cooking time: 9 mins
Preparation: 10 mins
K cal: 80/serve

Ingredients
A
**300 g (10 oz) Tientsin
    cabbage**
120 g (4 oz) sliced ham
5 red dates
1 cup chicken stock

1½ teaspoons cornstarch
1 tablespoon water

Preparation

Loosen leaves of the Tientsin cabbage, wash and cut into 4 cm (1½ in) lengths.

Cut each slice of ham into 6 pieces. Wash red dates and remove stone.

Mix cornstarch with 1 tablespoon water.

Cooking

Combine ingredients A in a 5 liter (5 qt) casserole. Cover and microwave on power **HIGH** for 8 minutes.

Stir in cornstarch mixture, cover and microwave on power **HIGH** for 1 minute.

Braised Vegetarian Mix

(photo page 89)

Serves 6
Cooking time: 9½ mins
Preparation: 15 mins
K cal: 100/serve

Ingredients
20 gingko nuts (*pak kor*)
6 red dates
20 dried golden lilies
6 dried black mushrooms
**50 g (2 oz) cellophane
    noodles**
**100 g (3½ oz) Tientsin
    cabbage**

A
**1½ pieces red fermented
    beancurd (*nam yee*)**
**1½ teaspoons chopped
    garlic**
1½ tablespoons oil

1 teaspoon sugar
1 cup water
½ teaspoon salt

Preparation

Shell gingko nuts, halve them and remove skin and bitter embryo in the center.

Wash red dates and discard stone. Soak dried golden lilies, dried black mushrooms and cellophane noodles.

Wash Tientsin cabbage and cut into 2 cm (1 in) lengths.

Cooking

Combine ingredients A in a 24 cm (9 in) casserole. Microwave on power **HIGH** for 3 minutes, uncovered.

Add remaining ingredients and mix evenly. Cover and microwave on power **HIGH** for 6½ minutes.

Broccoli Special

(photo page 81)

Serves 6
Cooking time: 7½ mins
Preparation: 15 mins
K cal: 125/serve

Ingredients

200 g (7 oz) broccoli
100 g (3½ oz) pork fillet
80 g (3 oz) pig's liver

A

1 teaspoon light soy sauce
½ teaspoon sugar
½ teaspoon cornstarch

B

1½ teaspoons chopped
    garlic
10 g (⅓ oz) young ginger,
    sliced finely
1 tablespoon oil

C

1 teaspoon salt
¼ cup water
1 teaspoon cornstarch
1 teaspoon wine

Preparation

Cut broccoli into florets. Slice pork fillet and season with ingredients A. Slice liver thin.

Cooking

Combine ingredients B in a 24 cm (9 in) casserole and microwave on power **HIGH** for 3 minutes, uncovered.

Add broccoli and seasoned pork fillet slices. Cover and microwave on power **HIGH** for 2 minutes.

Add liver slices and combined ingredients C. Cover and microwave on power **HIGH** for 2½ minutes.

Cabbage Rolls

(photo page 121)

Serves 4
Cooking time: 13 mins
Preparation: 15 mins
K cal: 220/serve

Ingredients

8 cabbage leaves, 250 g (9
    oz)

A

100 g (3½ oz) shrimp
100 g (3½ oz) lean pork
100 g (3½ oz) carrot
100 g (3½ oz) crab meat
1 teaspoon wine
2 teaspoons light soy sauce
1 teaspoon sesame oil
1 teaspoon sugar

B

1 teaspoon chopped shallot
1 tablespoon oil

Gravy

1 cup chicken stock
1½ teaspoons cornstarch

Garnish

2 cooked salted egg yolks, chopped coarsely

Preparation

Wash cabbage leaves. Shell and devein shrimp, then chop coarsely. Chop pork finely. Shred the carrot.

Cooking

Place cabbage leaves on a 32 cm (12 in) plate, cover with cling wrap and microwave on power **HIGH** for 2 minutes to soften leaves. Set aside.

Combine ingredients B in a small casserole. Microwave on power **HIGH** for 3½ minutes, uncovered. Add ingredients A and stir evenly. Microwave on power **HIGH** for 2½ minutes, uncovered.

Divide cooked ingredients into 8 portions and place a portion on each softened cabbage leaf. Wrap up cabbage leaves into rolls.

Place rolls on an oval plate, cover with cling wrap and microwave on power **HIGH** for 2½ minutes.

Combine gravy ingredients in a small casserole and microwave on power **HIGH** for 2½ minutes, uncovered.

Pour cooked gravy over cabbage rolls, top with chopped salted egg yolks and serve.

Cheong Meng Foo Kwai (Stuffed Pumpkin, p. 129)

Cheong Meng Foo Kwai (Stuffed Pumpkin)

(photo page 128)

Serves 10
Cooking time: 22 mins
Preparation: 20 mins
K cal: 185/serve

Ingredients
1 small pumpkin, 1⅕ kg (2
    lb 10 oz)
250 g (9 oz) lean pork
300 g (10 oz) shrimp,
    shelled
10 g (⅓ oz) Chinese parsley
1½ eggs, beaten

A
2 tablespoons light soy
    sauce
1 tablespoon sesame oil
½ teaspoon pepper
½ teaspoon five-spice
    powder
¼ teaspoon salt
½ teaspoon sugar

1 large carrot
10 dried black mushrooms

Gravy
1½ cups chicken stock
1½ tablespoons oyster
    sauce
½ teaspoon sugar
2 tablespoons light soy
    sauce

2½ teaspoons cornstarch

Garnish
10 quail's eggs, hardboiled

Preparation

Wash pumpkin and cut off a section ⅓ from the top. Scrape off the seeds.

Mince pork, shrimp, Chinese parsley and eggs with ingredients A into a paste. Place stuffing into the pumpkin.

Shape thick end of carrot into a tortoise head and the remaining sections into feet and a tail.

Soak dried black mushrooms to soften and drain off water.

Cooking

Place stuffed pumpkin in a 4 liter (4 qt) casserole and microwave on power MEDIUM–HIGH for 14 minutes, uncovered. Set aside.

Place shaped carrot tortoise head, feet and tail in a small plate and microwave on power HIGH for 1 minute, uncovered. Set aside.

Combine gravy ingredients with black mushrooms in a 24 cm (9 in) casserole and microwave on power HIGH for 6 minutes, uncovered.

Add cornstarch and microwave on power HIGH for 1 minute.

Assembly

Place cooked stuffed pumpkin on a serving plate with the skin side up, to resemble the shell of a tortoise. Place the carrot head, feet and tail in position with toothpicks.

Pour gravy mixture over pumpkin and garnish with quail's eggs surrounding tortoise.

Chung Hoe Prawns

(photo page 149)

Serves 6
Cooking time: 7 mins
Preparation: 15 mins
K cal: 55/serve

Ingredients
300 g (10 oz) chrysanthe-
    mum leaves (*chung hoe*)
150 g (5 oz) shrimp

A
3 slices young ginger
1 teaspoon chopped garlic
1 teaspoon chopped shallot
1½ tablespoons oil

1 tablespoon light soy sauce
½ teaspoon wine

Preparation

Wash chrysanthemum leaves and discard thick stems. Shell and devein shrimp.

Cooking

Combine ingredients A in a 3 liter (3 qt) casserole. Microwave on power HIGH for 3½ minutes, uncovered.

Add shrimp and microwave on power HIGH for 1 minute, uncovered.

Add remaining ingredients and cover. Microwave on power HIGH for 2½ minutes.

Diced Mixed Vegetables

Serves 6
Cooking time: 9 mins
Preparation: 15 mins
K cal: 255/serve

Ingredients
A

80 g (3 oz) salted radish
6 stalks long beans
80 g (3 oz) carrot
1 firm yellow beancurd
    square (*tau yoon*)
100 g (3½ oz) lean pork

B
1 red chile
4 cloves garlic
2 tablespoons oil

3 teaspoons light soy sauce
¼ cup water
½ cup roasted peanuts

Preparation
Dice ingredients A. Chop chile and garlic.

Cooking

Combine ingredients B in a 24 cm (9 in) casserole and microwave on power HIGH for 3 minutes, uncovered.

Add ingredients A, soy sauce and water. Cover and microwave on power HIGH for 6 minutes.

Stir in roasted peanuts and serve.

Eggplant with Minced Pork and Shrimp

Serves 6
Cooking time: 18 mins
Preparation: 15 mins
K cal: 140/serve

Ingredients
3 eggplants, 300 g (10 oz)
80 g (3 oz) shrimp
100 g (3½ oz) lean pork
2 tablespoons oil

A
6 cloves garlic, chopped
2 red chiles, chopped

1 tablespoon oyster sauce
¼ cup water

Preparation

Peel eggplants and cut into 5 cm (2 in) long strips.

Shell and devein shrimp and chop them with pork.

Cooking

Preheat a BROWNING DISH on power HIGH for 8 minutes.

Add oil and stir in eggplant strips. Cover and microwave on power HIGH for 3½ minutes.

Remove eggplant strips with a slotted spoon, leaving behind oil. Set aside the eggplant.

Add ingredients A to the oil and microwave on power HIGH for 3½ minutes, uncovered.

Add all other ingredients. Cover and microwave on power HIGH for 3 minutes. Stir when halfway through the cooking cycle.

Four Seasons with Scallops

(photo page 50)

Serves 10
Cooking time: 6 mins
Preparation: 10 mins
K cal: 25/serve

Ingredients
6 stalks asparagus
2 large tomatoes
24 young corn
2 teaspoons cornstarch
1 tablespoon water

A
4 red dates
3 dried scallops
1½ cups boiling water
20 straw mushrooms

Preparation

Cut each asparagus into 4 pieces. Wash and cut each tomato into 6 wedges.

Arrange on a serving plate in a circular pattern, 6 young corn alternating with 6 pieces of asparagus. Place tomato wedges in the center of the arrangement.

Mix cornstarch with 1 tablespoon water.

Wash red dates and remove the stone. Soak dried scallops and red dates in boiling hot water. Retain water to make gravy.

Cooking

Combine ingredients A in a small casserole. Cover and microwave on power HIGH for 3 minutes.

After 2 minutes of the cooking cycle, add cornstarch mixture to form gravy.

Pour gravy mixture over the vegetable arrangement.

Cover the serving plate with cling wrap and microwave on power HIGH for 3 minutes.

Jade and Ivory (p. 133), Teochew Duck (p. 102)

Jade and Ivory

(photo page 132)

Serves 10
Cooking time: 7 mins
Standing time: 5 mins
Preparation: 10 mins
K cal: 45/serve

Ingredients
200 g (7 oz) broccoli
200 g (7 oz) cauliflower

Gravy
150 g (5 oz) crabmeat
1 cup chicken stock
1 teaspoon salt
½ teaspoon sugar
1 teaspoon wine
1½ teaspoons cornstarch

1 egg, beaten

Preparation

Cut broccoli and cauliflower into florets and arrange them around a 32 cm (12 in) plate, alternating broccoli with cauliflower.

Cooking

Cover plate of broccoli and cauliflower with cling wrap. Microwave on power HIGH for 3½ minutes. Set aside.

Combine gravy ingredients in a small casserole. Cover and microwave on power HIGH for 3½ minutes.

Immediately after the cooking cycle, stir beaten egg into the gravy. Cover and let it STAND for 5 minutes.

Pour gravy over cooked vegetables and serve.

Lilies on Greens

(photo page 96)

Serves 6
Cooking time: 8 mins
Preparation: 15 mins
K cal: 130/serve

Ingredients
6 whole Taiwanese cabbages
80 g (3 oz) saltfish

A
100 g (3½ oz) fish fillet
100 g (3½ oz) belly pork
½ teaspoon salt

Gravy
1 cup chicken stock
1½ tablespoons light soy sauce
½ teaspoon wine
½ teaspoon sugar
1½ teaspoons cornstarch

Preparation

Wash Taiwanese cabbages carefully to ensure that stems are not broken off. Trim off the green leaves but do not discard them.

Slice saltfish thinly. Chop ingredients A together coarsely.

Cooking

Sandwich saltfish slices between paper towels and microwave on power HIGH for 3 minutes. Chop finely.

Mix half the saltfish with prepared ingredients A. Stuff this between stems of Taiwanese cabbages.

Place Taiwanese cabbage leaves on a plate and arrange stuffed stems on the leaves. Cover with cling wrap and microwave on power HIGH for 3 minutes.

Combine gravy ingredients in a small casserole and microwave on power HIGH for 2 minutes, uncovered.

Pour gravy over the cooked vegetables and sprinkle with remaining saltfish. Serve immediately.

Lotus Pond

Serves 6
Cooking time: 8½ mins
Preparation: 15 mins
K cal: 135/serve

Ingredients
200 g (7 oz) lotus root
100 g (3½ oz) onion
100 g (3½ oz) lean pork

A
1 teaspoon wine
1¼ tablespoons light soy
    sauce
½ teaspoon sugar
2 teaspoons cornstarch

10 red dates
½ cup chicken stock
1½ tablespoons oil

Preparation

Cut lotus root into thin slices and the onion into wedges.

Slice pork into strips and marinate with combined ingredients A. Soak red dates and discard stone.

Cooking

Combine onion wedges, pork strips and oil in a 3 liter (3 qt) casserole. Microwave on power HIGH for 3½ minutes, uncovered.

Add remaining ingredients and mix evenly. Cover and microwave on power HIGH for 5 minutes.

Stir halfway through the cooking cycle.

Mushroom Medley

(photo page 124)

Serves 10
Cooking time: 8½ mins
Preparation: 10 mins
K cal: 40/serve

Ingredients
15 small dried black
    mushrooms
100 g (3½ oz) fresh abalone
    mushrooms
15 button mushrooms
15 straw mushrooms
100 g (3½ oz) spring
    onions

A
1 teaspoon chopped garlic
2 teaspoons chopped shallot
1 tablespoon oil

B
1 teaspoon wine
¼ cup chicken stock
1 tablespoon oyster sauce
1 teaspoon cornstarch

Garnish
100 g (3½ oz) toasted peanuts

Preparation

Soak dried black mushrooms to soften, then drain off water. Cut abalone mushrooms into 2 cm (1 in) cubes. The other mushrooms are left whole.

Wash and cut spring onions into 4 cm (1½ in) lengths.

Cooking

Combine ingredients A in a 24 cm (9 in) casserole and microwave on power HIGH for 3 minutes, uncovered.

Add abalone and black mushrooms and stir to coat evenly with oil. Microwave on power HIGH for 2 minutes, uncovered.

Add button and straw mushrooms and ingredients B. Cover and microwave on power HIGH for 3½ minutes.

Add spring onions, cover and let casserole STAND for 5 minutes.

Stir in toasted peanuts and serve.

Nam Yee Foong Kong (Fried Water Convolvulus)

Serves 6
Cooking time: 6 mins
Preparation: 10 mins
K cal: 50/serve

Ingredients
300 g (10 oz) water convolvulus
1 piece red fermented beancurd (*nam yee*)
1½ teaspoons chopped garlic
1 teaspoon sugar
1½ tablespoons oil

Preparation

Clean water convolvulus and cut into 5 cm (2 in) lengths.

Mash red fermented beancurd.

Cooking

Combine all ingredients except water convolvulus in a 24 cm (9 in) casserole and microwave on power HIGH for 3½ minutes, uncovered.

Add water convolvulus and stir to coat with cooked ingredients. Cover and microwave on power HIGH for 2½ minutes.

NOTE: *Water convolvulus is cultivated on land and grows wild in water. This particular recipe uses the cultivated variety; its stems are finer. For salads, the coarser water-grown variety is used.*

Salad Cup

(photo page 47)

Serves 10
Cooking time: 9 mins
Preparation: 15 mins
K cal: 80/serve

Ingredients
20 lettuce leaves

A
200 g (7 oz) yam bean
100 g (3½ oz) carrot
15 French beans
100 g (3½ oz) belly pork
20 g (¾ oz) dried cuttlefish strips
¼ cup water
3 teaspoons light soy sauce

½ tablespoon chopped shallots
1 tablespoon oil

Dip
hoisin **sauce with mustard**

Preparation

Wash lettuce leaves, taking care not to tear them. Refrigerate leaves in a plastic bag to crisp.

Shred yam bean, carrot and French beans. Cut belly pork into thin strips.

Soak dried cuttlefish strips in ¼ cup water and retain water for cooking.

Cooking

Combine chopped shallots with oil in a 5 liter (5 qt) casserole and microwave on power HIGH for 3 minutes, uncovered.

Add ingredients A, cover the casserole and microwave on power HIGH for 6 minutes.

Arrange lettuce leaves on a serving plate and fill them with the cooked ingredients.

Serve with *hoisin* sauce and mustard.

Salted Mustard Cabbage and Pig's Feet

Serves 10
Cooking time: 50 mins
Preparation: 10 mins
K cal: 125/serve

Ingredients
800 g (1 lb 12 oz) roasted
    pig's feet
250 g (9 oz) salted mustard
    cabbage (leafy variety)
150 g (5 oz) tomatoes
3 red chiles
100 g (3½ oz) belly pork
2 pieces dried tamarind
1½ cups water
½ teaspoon sugar
½ teaspoon salt

Preparation

Ask your butcher to chop pig's feet into serving portions.

Wash salted mustard cabbage to remove excess salt and slice finely. Cut tomatoes into wedges. Wash chiles, remove seeds and halve them.

Slice belly pork into thin pieces.

Cooking

Combine all ingredients in a 5 liter (5 qt) casserole. Cover the casserole and microwave on power HIGH for 5 minutes.

Next, simmer on power MEDIUM-LOW for 45 minutes, still covered.

Let the casserole STAND for 15 minutes before serving.

NOTE: *This casserole is best cooked in the morning and eaten during the evening meal. Roasted pig's feet can be replaced by leftover roast chicken.*

Salted Vegetable

Cooking time: 10 mins
Preparation: 10 mins
K cal: 280

Ingredients
600 g (1 lb 5 oz) mustard
    cabbage

A
2 liters (2 qt) rice water★
4 pieces dried tamarind
3 tablespoons salt
2 tablespoons brown sugar

★ *Rice water is the water used to rinse uncooked rice. Usually the first rinse is discarded, the second rinse used.*

Preparation

Wash mustard cabbage under running water, keeping the whole plant intact.

Dry and soften vegetable under mid-morning sun for 2 hours.

Cooking

Combine ingredients A in a 4 liter (4 qt) casserole and microwave on power HIGH for 10 minutes, uncovered.

When rice water mixture has cooled, pour it into an earthen container with mustard cabbage. Cover the container and allow the vegetable to mature for 3 weeks. Turn the vegetable over once a week.

After 3 weeks, remove salted mustard cabbage from earthen container. Refrigerate and use as required.

Sam See Chap Choy (Shredded Mixed Vegetable, p. 138)

Sam See Chap Choy (Shredded Mixed Vegetables) *(photo page 137)*

Serves 6
Cooking time: 6 mins
Preparation: 15 mins
K cal: 180/serve

Ingredients
80 g (3 oz) cucumber
6 dried black mushrooms
100 g (3½ oz) carrot
80 g (3 oz) Chinese celery
150 g (5 oz) belly pork
5 g (⅕ oz) agar strips

A
1 teaspoon chopped garlic
1 tablespoon oil

B
1 teaspoon sesame oil
1 tablespoon plum sauce
1 tablespoon oyster sauce
1 teaspoon brown sugar

Garnish
2 tablespoons toasted
    sesame seeds

Preparation

Remove seeds from cucumber. Soak dried black mushrooms to soften, then drain off water.

Cut cucumber, mushrooms, carrot, celery and belly pork into strips. Cut agar strips into 4 cm (1½ in) lengths.

Cooking

Combine ingredients A with mushroom and pork strips in a 24 cm (9 in) casserole. Microwave on power HIGH for 3½ minutes, uncovered.

Add the remaining ingredients (except the sesame seeds) and microwave on power HIGH for 2½ minutes, still uncovered.

Sprinkle with toasted sesame seeds and serve.

Sautéed Chives with Seafood *(photo page 78)*

Serves 6
Cooking time: 7 mins
Preparation: 15 mins
K cal: 90/serve

Ingredients
200 g (7 oz) flowering
    chives
1 onion
1 teaspoon cornstarch
1 tablespoon water

A
100 g (3½ oz) prawns
3 cuttlefish
1½ teaspoons light soy
    sauce
½ teaspoon salt
½ teaspoon sugar

1 tablespoon oil

Preparation

Wash flowering chives and cut into 3 cm (1 in) lengths. Slice the onion. Mix cornstarch with 1 tablespoon water.

Shell and devein prawns. Clean and cut cuttlefish into bite-sized pieces.

Cooking

Combine onion slices with oil in 24 cm (9 in) casserole and microwave on power HIGH for 3 minutes, uncovered.

Stir in ingredients A and microwave on power HIGH for 1½ minutes, uncovered.

Add flowering chives and the cornstarch mixture. Cover and microwave on power HIGH for 2½ minutes.

Shredded Cucumber with Cellophane Noodles

Serves 6
Cooking time: 8½ mins
Preparation: 10 mins
K cal: 70/serve

Ingredients

180 g (6 oz) cucumber
30 g (1 oz) cellophane
   noodles
20 g (¾ oz) dried sweet
   beancurd sheets (*tim
   chook*)

A
20 g (¾ oz) dried shrimp
1 teaspoon chopped onion
1 tablespoon oil

2 teaspoons light soy sauce
1½ cups water

Preparation

Wash and shred the cucumber. Soak cellophane noodles to soften, then drain off water. Wash dried sweet beancurd sheets and cut into strips.

Wash dried shrimp and chop coarsely.

Cooking

Combine ingredients A in a 24 cm (9 in) casserole and microwave on power HIGH for 3 minutes, uncovered.

Add remaining ingredients, cover and microwave on power HIGH for 5½ minutes.

Snow Peas with Beef

(photo page 109)

Serves 6
Cooking time: 7 mins
Preparation: 10 mins
K cal: 65/serve

Ingredients

50 g (1½ oz) carrot
100 g (3½ oz) onion
100 g (3½ oz) beef

A
1 teaspoon light soy sauce
1 teaspoon ginger juice
1 teaspoon cooked oil
dash of baking soda

½ tablespoon oil
150 g (5 oz) snow peas
½ teaspoon light soy sauce

Preparation

Slice carrot thinly. Cut onion into wedges.

Slice beef thinly and season with ingredients A.

Cooking

Combine onion wedges with oil in a 24 cm (9 in) shallow casserole and microwave on power HIGH for 2½ minutes, uncovered.

Add carrot and seasoned beef. Cover and microwave on power HIGH for 3 minutes.

Add snow peas and stir in light soy sauce. Cover and microwave on power HIGH for 1½ minutes.

Yam Cake (p. 177), Black Bean Spare Ribs (p. 64), Siew Mai (p. 174)

Soybean Sprouts with Minced Meat

Serves 6
Cooking time: 11 mins
Preparation: 10 mins
K cal: 100/serve

Ingredients
200 g (7 oz) soybean
    sprouts
½ tablespoon chopped
    shallot
1 tablespoon oil
100 g (3½ oz) minced pork
1 tablespoon oyster sauce
¼ cup water

Preparation

Wash and remove 'tails' of soybean sprouts. Chop soybean sprouts finely.

Cooking

Combine chopped shallots with oil in a 24 cm (9 in) casserole and microwave on power HIGH for 3 minutes, uncovered.

Add soybean sprouts and minced pork and microwave on power HIGH for 3 minutes, still uncovered.

Add oyster sauce and water. Cover and microwave on power HIGH for 5 minutes.

Spicy Asparagus

(photo page 43)

Serves 6
Cooking time: 7 mins
Preparation: 10 mins
K cal: 90/serve

Ingredients
300 g (10 oz) asparagus

A
30 g (1 oz) dried shrimp
10 shallots
4 cloves garlic
30 g (1 oz) red chiles
1 teaspoon hot bean sauce

B
2 tablespoons oil
1 teaspoon sugar

Preparation

Wash and cut asparagus into 4 cm (1½ in) lengths.

Wash and soak dried shrimp. Chop combined ingredients A finely.

Cooking

Combine chopped ingredients A with ingredients B in a 24 cm (9 in) casserole and microwave on power HIGH for 4 minutes, uncovered.

Add asparagus and mix evenly. Cover and microwave on power HIGH for 3 minutes.

Spinach with Prawn Sauce

(photo page 34)

Serves 6
Cooking time: 8 mins
Preparation: 10 mins
K cal: 50/serve

Ingredients
200 g (7 oz) spinach
1 teaspoon chopped garlic
1 tablespoon oil

A
80 g (3 oz) shrimp, minced
½ teaspoon salt
1 teaspoon light soy sauce
½ cup water
1 teaspoon cornstarch

1 egg, beaten

Preparation

Wash and cut spinach into 5 cm (2 in) lengths. Separate stems from leaves. Place spinach leaves in the center of plate and the stems surrounding the leaves.

Cooking

Cover the plate of spinach with cling wrap and microwave on power HIGH for 2 minutes. Set aside.

Combine garlic and oil in a small casserole and microwave on power HIGH for 3 minutes, uncovered.

Add ingredients A and microwave on power HIGH for 3 minutes, uncovered. Stir beaten egg into prawn sauce.

Pour cooked prawn sauce over cooked spinach and serve.

Spring Garlic with Beancurd

Serves 6
Cooking time: 8½ mins
Preparation: 10 mins
K cal: 85/serve

Ingredients
12 spring garlic shoots
20 g (½ oz) carrot
200 g (7 oz) prawns

A
2 pieces firm white
    beancurd squares (*tau foo*)
1 big onion
1 tablespoon oil

2 tablespoons water
1 teaspoon salt
½ teaspoon sugar

Preparation

Cut spring garlic shoots to 3 cm (1 in) lengths. Slice carrot thinly. Shell and devein prawns.

Cut firm beancurd into ½ cm (¼ in) thick slices. Peel and cut onion into wedges.

Cooking

Combine ingredients A in a 24 cm (9 in) shallow casserole and microwave on power HIGH for 4 minutes, uncovered.

Add remaining ingredients, stir to ensure even coating with ingredients A and cover the casserole.

Microwave on power HIGH for 4½ minutes. Stir halfway through the cooking cycle.

Stir-fried Leek

(photo page 116)

Serves 6
Cooking time: 8 mins
Standing time: 5 mins
Preparation: 10 mins
K cal: 120/serve

Ingredients
A
200 g (7 oz) leek
150 g (5 oz) roast pork
2 teaspoons light soy sauce
¼ teaspoon dark soy sauce
½ teaspoon sugar

B
1 big onion, cut into
**   wedges**
3 slices ginger
1 teaspoon chopped garlic
1½ tablespoons oil

Preparation

Wash leek and cut diagonally into 2 cm (1 in) lengths. Cut roast pork into 1 cm (½ in) thick slices.

Cooking

Combine ingredients B in a 24 cm (9 in) shallow casserole and microwave on power **HIGH** for 4 minutes, uncovered.

Add ingredients A and stir to ensure even coating with ingredients B. Cover the casserole and microwave on power **HIGH** for 4 minutes.

Stir ingredients halfway through the cooking cycle. Let the casserole **STAND** for 5 minutes before serving.

Stuffed Eggplant

(photo page 55)

Serves 6
Cooking time: 14½ mins
Standing time: 10 mins
Preparation: 15 mins
K cal: 100/serve

Ingredients
3 eggplants, 300 g (10 oz)

A
30 g (1 oz) dried shrimp
1½ tablespoons preserved
**   soy beans**
1 red chile
4 cloves garlic
6 shallots

2 teaspoons sugar
2 tablespoons oil
3 tablespoons water

toothpicks

Preparation

Leaving either end intact, slit each eggplant lengthwise, about ²/₃ deep, to form a pocket.

Soak dried shrimp to soften, then drain them. Chop ingredients A till fine and mix with sugar and ½ tablespoon oil.

Cooking

Combine ingredients A in a small casserole and microwave on power **HIGH** for 3½ minutes, uncovered.

Stir in water and divide cooked ingredients into 3 portions.

Stuff each portion of cooked ingredients into the pocket of each eggplant. Secure with toothpicks.

Preheat a **BROWNING DISH** on power **HIGH** for 6 minutes.

Pour in 1½ tablespoons oil and place stuffed eggplants on the dish, turning so as to cook both sides.

Cover the browning dish and microwave on power **HIGH** for 5 minutes.

Let the dish **STAND** for 10 minutes, covered, before serving.

Stuffed Green Peppers

(photo page 29)

Serves 6
Cooking time: 7½ mins
Preparation: 20 mins
K cal: 165/serve

Ingredients

3 green peppers, 300 g (10 oz)
30 g (1 oz) carrot

A
150 g (5 oz) belly pork
150 g (5 oz) fish fillet
2 teaspoons cornstarch
1 teaspoon salt

B
5 slices young ginger
1 tablespoon oyster sauce
1 cup chicken stock
1½ teaspoons cornstarch
1 teaspoon wine

Preparation

Halve green peppers crosswise and remove seeds. Chop carrot finely.

Chop ingredients A together to a paste. Mix chopped carrots with ingredients A and divide into 6 portions. Stuff 1 portion into each green pepper half.

Cooking

Place stuffed green peppers on a 32 cm (12 in) plate. Cover with cling wrap and microwave on power MEDIUM for 5 minutes. Set aside.

Combine ingredients B in a small casserole. Microwave on power HIGH for 2½ minutes, uncovered, to make gravy.

Pour gravy over the cooked stuffed peppers and serve.

Stuffed Hairy Marrow

(photo page 112)

Serves 6
Cooking time: 7 mins
Preparation: 15 mins
K cal: 85/serve

Ingredients

1 hairy marrow, 200 g (7 oz)
2 teaspoons cornstarch
1½ tablespoons water

A
150 g (5 oz) shrimp
100 g (3½ oz) lean pork
½ teaspoon salt
½ teaspoon sugar
dash of pepper

1 cup chicken stock

Preparation

Scrape off skin of hairy marrow and cut vegetable into 3 cm (1 in) thick round slices. Remove pulp from the center.

Mix cornstarch with 1½ tablespoons water.

Shell and devein shrimp. Combine ingredients A and chop fine for stuffing.

Fill the central space of the marrow pieces with stuffing.

Cooking

Arrange stuffed marrow pieces in a 2 liter (2 qt) oval casserole. Pour chicken stock over the vegetable. Cover casserole with cling wrap and microwave on power HIGH for 7 minutes.

After 5½ minutes of the cooking cycle, stir in the cornstarch mixture, then resume the cycle.

Sweet and Sour Vegetables

Serves 6
Cooking time: 12½ mins
Preparation: 10 mins
K cal: 130/serve

Ingredients
200 g (7 oz) salted mustard
　　cabbage
100 g (3½ oz) belly pork
1 teaspoon cornstarch
⅓ cup water

A
1 red chile, chopped
2 teaspoons chopped garlic
1½ tablespoons oil

2 teaspoons sugar
1 teaspoon light soy sauce

Preparation

Wash salted mustard cabbage to remove excess salt and slice finely. Cut belly pork into strips.

Mix cornstarch with 1 tablespoon water.

Cooking

Sandwich sliced mustard cabbage between paper towels and microwave on power HIGH for 3 minutes to dry.

Combine ingredients A in a 24 cm (9 in) shallow casserole and microwave on power HIGH for 3 minutes, uncovered.

Add salted mustard cabbage, belly pork and sugar. Microwave on power HIGH for 3 minutes, uncovered.

Stir in light soy sauce and the remaining water. Cover and microwave on power HIGH for 3½ minutes.

After 2 minutes of the cooking cycle, stir in cornstarch mixture, then resume cooking.

Szechuan Mixed Vegetables

(photo page 124)

Serves 10
Cooking time: 11 mins
Preparation: 10 mins
K cal: 55/serve

Ingredients
A
200 g (7 oz) Tientsin
　　cabbage
100 g (3½ oz) carrot
2 sticks dried beancurd (*foo
　　chook*)
100 g (3½ oz) button
　　mushrooms
20 straw mushrooms

B
1½ teaspoons chopped
　　garlic
2 teaspoons hot bean sauce
1 teaspoon sugar
1½ tablespoons oil

¼ cup water
20 snow peas

Preparation

Wash and cut Tientsin cabbage into 3 cm (1 in) pieces. Cut carrot into thin slices. Soak dried beancurd sticks.

Cooking

Combine ingredients B in a 5 liter (5 qt) casserole and microwave on power HIGH for 3 minutes, uncovered.

Add ingredients A and water. Cover and microwave on power HIGH for 8 minutes.

After 6 minutes of the cooking cycle, add snow peas, then resume the cycle.

Vegetable Omelette Soufflé

Serves 6
Cooking time: 10½ mins
Preparation: 15 mins
K cal: 80/serve

Ingredients
3 eggs

A
50 g (1½ oz) carrot
60 g (2 oz) onion
100 g (3½ oz) button
   mushrooms
100 g (3½ oz) green peas
1 tablespoon oyster sauce
3 tablespoons water

1 tablespoon oil

Preparation

Separate egg yolks from whites. Beat the yolks. Whisk egg whites till fluffy and fold in beaten egg yolks.

Dice carrot, onion and button mushrooms.

Cooking

Combine ingredients A in a small casserole. Cover and microwave on power **HIGH** for 3 minutes.

Preheat a **BROWNING DISH** on power **HIGH** for 6 minutes.

Add oil and pour in the egg mixture. Place cooked ingredients on top of egg mixture. Microwave on power **HIGH** for 1½ minutes, uncovered.

Loosen the omelette from the bottom of the dish and fold carefully in half so as not to break it.

Watercress with Fresh Oysters

(photo page 59)

Serves 6
Cooking time: 6½ mins
Preparation: 10 mins
K cal: 75/serve

Ingredients
300 g (10 oz) watercress
150 g (5 oz) fresh oysters
1½ tablespoons chopped
   garlic
2 tablespoons oil
1 tablespoon light soy sauce

Preparation

Wash watercress and, using only young shoots and leaves, cut into 4 cm (1½ in) lengths. Arrange watercress and fresh oysters on a 32 cm (12 in) plate.

Cooking

Combine chopped garlic with oil in a small casserole. Microwave on power **HIGH** for 3½ minutes, uncovered.

Pour cooked mixture over the watercress and oyster arrangement and sprinkle with light soy sauce. Cover the plate with cling wrap and microwave on power **HIGH** for 3 minutes.

Winter Delight

(photo page 67)

Serves 6
Cooking time: 9 mins
Preparation: 15 mins
K cal: 130/serve

Ingredients
200 g (7 oz) winter melon
100 g (3½ oz) broccoli
    stems
10 pieces deep-fried
    beancurd balls (*tau foo
    pok*)

A
10 small dried black
    muchrooms
½ tablespoon chopped
    onion
1 tablespoon oil

½ cup chicken stock
1½ tablespoons light soy
    sauce
1 teaspoon wine
½ teaspoon sugar

Garnish
1 tablespoon toasted fish

Preparation

Scrape off skin of winter melon. With a sharp knife, cut slices about 1 cm (½ in) thick. Use a cookie cutter to cut out floral shapes.

Peel skin of broccoli stems. Slice stems to ½ cm (¼ in) thickness, and similarly cut out floral shapses.

Halve deep-fried beancurd balls. Soak dried black mushrooms to soften.

Cooking

Combine ingredients A in a 3 liter (3 qt) casserole. Microwave on power HIGH for 4 minutes, uncovered.

Add remaining ingredients (except the garnish) and mix evenly. Cover and microwave on power HIGH for 5 minutes.

Garnish with toasted fish and serve.

Yoke Mooi Choy

Serves 6
Cooking time: 12 mins
Preparation: 10 mins
K cal: 170/serve

Ingredients
150 g (5 oz) sweet *mooi choy*
1½ teaspoons cornstarch
1 cup water

A
150 g (5 oz) belly pork
1½ teaspoons chopped
    garlic
1 tablespoon oil

Preparation

Wash sweet *mooi choy* under running water, drain and cut into 1 cm (½ in) lengths. Mix cornstarch with 1 tablespoon water.

Cut belly pork into strips.

Cooking

Combine ingredients A in a 24 cm (9 in) casserole and microwave on power HIGH for 4 minutes, uncovered.

Add *mooi choy* and the remaining water. Cover the casserole and microwave on power HIGH for 8 minutes.

After 6 minutes of the cooking cycle, add the cornstarch mixture, then resume the cycle.

RICE

'A gourmet will eat plain rice and not ask for other food.'

To appreciate the natural sweetness of rice, it has to be cooked with just the right amount of water so that the cooked texture is chewable, not hard and grainy (just undercooked) or too soft (overcooked with excess water).

Rice cooks perfectly in the microwave oven, each grain separate from the next, so that in both presentation and taste, the gourmet would be satisfied. Cover the cooking container and give it two or three minutes of standing time to allow the grains to fluff out after cooking.

It is natural that, eating it daily, the Chinese should have found some cures in rice. Boiled burnt rice is believed to be a digestive aid and plain rice porridge brings relief for sufferers of diarrhea and vomiting.

Claypot Chicken Rice *150*
Ginger Beef Rice *150*
Lotus Leaf Rice *151*
Paddy Frog Porridge *151*

Lotus Leaf Rice (p. 151), Chung Hoe Prawns (p. 130)

Claypot Chicken Rice

Serves 6
Cooking time: 18 mins
Preparation: 20 mins
K cal: 320/serve

Ingredients
300 g (10 oz) long-grain
    rice
60 g (2 oz) Chinese sau-
    sages
10 g (⅓ oz) saltfish
300 g (10 oz) chicken fillet

A
1 tablespoon oyster sauce
2 tablespoons light soy
    sauce
1 teaspoon dark soy sauce
1½ teaspoons wine
1 teaspoon ginger juice
1½ tablespoons cooked oil

1⅓ cups water

Preparation

Wash rice in a strainer.

Slice Chinese sausages thinly. Chop saltfish coarsely.

Cut chicken into 3 cm (1 in) cubes and season with combined ingredients A.

Cooking

Place rice and water in a 3 liter (3 qt) casserole. Microwave on power
HIGH for 12 minutes, uncovered.

Stir rice before placing seasoned chicken cubes, Chinese sausage
slices and saltfish on top of rice.

Cover and microwave on power MEDIUM for 6 minutes.

NOTE: *An incredibly fast and easy one-pot lunch or dinner when required in a
hurry.*

Ginger Beef Rice

Serves 4
Cooking time: 18 mins
Preparation: 15 mins
K cal: 435/serve

Ingredients
200 g (7 oz) beef, tender
    cut
300 g (10 oz) long-grain
    rice

A
1½ tablespoons light soy
    sauce
1 teaspoon dark soy sauce
⅛ teaspoon baking soda
1 teaspoon sesame oil

B
60 g (2 oz) young ginger,
    sliced finely
2 teaspoons chopped garlic
2 tablespoons oil

1⅓ cups water

Preparation

Slice beef thinly and season with combined ingredients A. Wash rice
in a strainer.

Cooking

Combine ingredients B in a 3 liter (3 qt) casserole. Microwave on
power HIGH for 4 minutes, uncovered.

Add rice and water. Cover and microwave on power HIGH for 10
minutes.

Stir rice before placing seasoned beef slices on top of it. Cover and
microwave on power MEDIUM for 4 minutes.

NOTE: *This used to be my mother's favorite packed school lunch for my siblings
and me.*

Lotus Leaf Rice

(photo page 149)

Serves 10
Cooking time: 21½ mins
Preparation: 20 mins
K cal: 180/serve

Ingredients
200 g (7 oz) long-grain rice
1 big lotus leaf

A
50 g (1½ oz) dried shrimp
15 g (½ oz) dried cuttlefish
   strips
100 g (3½ oz) lean pork
4 dried black mushrooms,
   soaked
30 g (1 oz) Chinese sau-
   sages

B
1 teaspoon chopped garlic
2 teaspoons chopped
   shallots
2 tablespoons oil

C
1 tablespoon light soy sauce
1 teaspoon wine
1 teaspoon sesame oil
1 teaspoon dark soy sauce

¾ cup water
1 cup hot water

Preparation

Wash rice in a stainer and soak in clean water for 1 hour. Wipe lotus leaf clean with a wet cloth.

Wash dried shrimp and cuttlefish strips and drain dry. Dice lean pork, softened black mushrooms and Chinese sausages.

Cooking

Combine ingredients B in a 24 cm (9 in) casserole. Microwave on power HIGH for 3½ minutes, uncovered.

Add ingredients A and C, mixing evenly. Microwave on power HIGH for 2 minutes, uncovered.

Add rice and ¾ cup water. Microwave on power HIGH for 6 minutes, uncovered. Set aside.

Place lotus leaf in a 5 liter (5 qt) casserole. Put cooked ingredients in the center of the leaf and wrap, envelope style. Pour 1 cup hot water in the casserole. Cover and microwave on power MEDIUM for 10 minutes.

Unwrap the lotus leaf and scoop out cooked rice to serve.

NOTE: *If fresh lotus leaves are not available, use dried ones. Just soak in water for 5–10 minutes before use*

Paddy Frog Porridge

Serves 4
Cooking time: 30 mins
Preparation: 15 mins
K cal: 190/serve

Ingredients
100 g (3½ oz) broken rice
300 g (10 oz) paddy frog's
   legs

A
30 g (1 oz) young ginger,
   shredded
1 teaspoon sesame oil
¼ teaspoon pepper
1 tablespoon cooked oil
1½ teaspoons salt

4 cups water

Preparation

Wash rice in a strainer till clean. Stir in 1 teaspoon of the oil from ingredients A.

Wash frog's legs and season with combined ingredients A.

Cooking

Combine prepared rice with 2 cups water in a 5 liter (5 qt) casserole. Microwave on power HIGH for 10 minutes, uncovered.

Add remaining water. Cover and microwave on power MEDIUM for 15 minutes.

Add seasoned frog's legs. Cover and microwave on power HIGH for 5 minutes.

NOTE: *This is an ideal food for breakfast, or lunch on a hot afternoon.*

Sea Kingdom (p. 157), Sweet Sour Crabs (p. 60)

NOODLES

Noodles may be said to be Asia's convenience food, fast to cook, wholesome if you add a few slices of meat and some leafy vegetables. Cook as you would on a conventional stove, with an eye to the correct texture or elasticity of the strands.

Noodles are added at the last cooking stage in the microwave oven. All other ingredients are cooked first. By the time noodles are added, the gravy or stock is rapidly boiling and it requires only a few minutes before the strands are just cooked. Standing time is necessary to bring the noodles to the correct texture.

More detailed notes on the cooking method for different noodles, as well as their composition, are given in the notes on ingredients at the beginning of the book.

Birthday Noodles

Serves 6
Cooking time: 11 mins
Standing time: 10 mins
Preparation: 15 mins
K cal: 160/serve

Ingredients
200 g (7 oz) *wonton* noodles

A
8 dried black mushrooms
100 g (3½ oz) deep-fried
   fish cakes
10 g (⅓ oz) dried sweet
   beancurd sheets (*tim
   chook*)
1 tablespoon oyster sauce
1 teaspoon light soy sauce
1 teaspoon dark soy sauce
½ cup chicken stock

B
80 g (3 oz) Tientsin cab-
   bage
50 g (1½ oz) carrot
80 g (3 oz) beansprouts

C
2 teaspoons chopped shallot
1½ tablespoons oil

Preparation

Lightly wash wonton noodles with hot water and drain.

Soak dried black mushrooms and when softened, slice thinly. Cut fish cakes and dried sweet beancurd sheets into strips. Shred Tientsin cabbage and carrot. Wash and pluck off 'tails' of beansprouts.

Cooking

Combine ingredients C in a 2 liter (2 qt) shallow casserole. Microwave on power high for 3½ minutes, uncovered.

Add ingredients A and microwave on power HIGH for 1½ minutes, uncovered.

Add noodles and stir. Cover and microwave on power HIGH for 6 minutes. Stir again after 2 minutes of the cooking cycle.

Immediately after the cooking cycle, add ingredients B and stir evenly. Cover and let casserole STAND for 10 minutes before serving.

NOTE: *The Cantonese name for this dish is Sam See Meen. Noodles are customarily served when celebrating a birthday. The long strands are not easily broken, signifying a long and peaceful life.*

Claypot Crab Fun See

Serves 2
Cooking time: 9½ mins
Standing time: 10 mins
Preparation: 10 mins
K cal: 660/serve

Ingredients
100 g (3½ oz) cellophane
   noodles
6 crab claws, 250 g (9 oz)
100 g (3½ oz) pork fat
100 g (3½ oz) Tientsin
   cabbage

A
½ cup fish stock
½ teaspoon dark soy sauce
½ teaspoon oyster sauce

Preparation

Wash noodles and soak in combined ingredients A.

Wash and crack crab claws. Slice pork fat thinly into 6 cm (2½ in) squares. Cut Tientsin cabbage into 1 cm (½ in) lengths.

Cooking

Line a 3 liter (3 qt) claypot with slices of pork fat. Microwave on power HIGH for 1½ minutes, uncovered.

Add the remaining ingredients. Cover and microwave on power MEDIUM for 8 minutes.

Let claypot STAND covered for 10 minutes.

Claypot Prawn Noodles

Serves 2
Cooking time: 15 mins
Standing time: 10 mins
Preparation: 15 mins
K cal: 460/serve

Ingredients
300 g (10 oz) freshwater
    prawns
100 g (3½ oz) Taiwanese
    cabbage

A
½ teaspoon chopped garlic
1½ tablespoons oil

B
3 cups chicken stock
1 tablespoon oyster sauce

150 g (5 oz) deep-fried
    noodles
1 egg, beaten

Preparation

Clean prawns, trim whiskers and slice in half lengthwise

Separate leaves of Taiwanese cabbage and wash under running water.

Cooking

Combine ingredients A in a 3 liter (3 qt) claypot. Microwave on power **HIGH** for 3 minutes, uncovered.

Add ingredients B, cover and microwave on power **HIGH** for 7 minutes. Add prawns and noodles. Cover and microwave on power **HIGH** for 5 minutes.

Immediately after the cooking cycle, stir in Taiwanese cabbage and beaten egg. Cover and let claypot **STAND** for 10 minutes before serving.

Fish Head Rice Noodles

Serves 4
Cooking time: 21 mins
Standing time: 10 mins
Preparation: 10 mins
K cal: 310/serve

Ingredients
150 g (5 oz) thin rice
    noodles
500 g (1 lb 1 oz) red
    snapper head

A
10 g (⅓ oz) ginger slices
2 tablespoons oil

B
60 g (2 oz) bitter gourd,
    sliced thinly
4 cups fish stock
1 teaspoon light soy sauce
1 teaspoon salt

30 g (1 oz) lard crisps

Preparation

Soak rice noodles to soften and discard water. Fish head should be in pieces.

Cooking

Preheat a **BROWNING DISH** on power **HIGH** for 8 minutes.

Add ingredients A and fish head pieces. Microwave on power **HIGH** for 3 minutes, uncovered.

Add ingredients B, cover and microwave on power **HIGH** for 10 minutes. After 7 minutes of the cooking cycle, add rice noodles.

Cover and let **STAND** for 10 minutes. Stir in lard crisps and serve.

NOTE: *The Cantonese name for this dish is Yee Tow Mai.*

Fried Fun See

Serves 4
Cooking time: 9½ mins
Standing time: 10 mins
Preparation: 15 mins
K cal: 170/serve

Ingredients

80 g (3 oz) cellophane
    noodles
100 g (3½ oz) Tientsin
    cabbage
100 g (3½ oz) chicken fillet
10 g (⅓ oz) wood ear
    fungus (*mook yee*)

A

4 dried black mushrooms
1½ teaspoons chopped
    garlic
1½ tablespoons oil

1 cup chicken stock
1 tablespoon light soy sauce
½ teaspoon dark soy sauce

Preparation

Wash and soak cellophane noodles. Drain off water when softened.

Cut Tientsin cabbage into ½ cm (¼ in) lengths. Cut chicken into strips.

Soak wood ears and dried black mushrooms to soften, then slice thinly.

Cooking

Combine ingredients A in a 2 liter (2 qt) shallow casserole. Microwave on power HIGH for 3½ minutes, uncovered.

Add remaining ingredients, cover and microwave on power HIGH for 6 minutes.

Let casserole STAND for 10 minutes before serving.

Fried Noodles (Char Cheong Meen)

(photo page 62)

Serves 6
Cooking time: 13½ mins
Standing time: 10 mins
Preparation: 15 mins
K cal: 205/serve

Ingredients

200 g (7 oz) thick yellow
    noodles
2 teaspoons cornstarch
1½ cups chicken stock

A

5 dried black mushrooms
50 g (1½ oz) Szechuan
    vegetable
50 g (1½ oz) carrot
50 g (1½ oz) firm white
    beancurd squares (*tau
    foo*)
100 g (3½ oz) lean pork
1 teaspoon dark soy sauce

B

1 teaspoon chopped garlic
1 teaspoon chopped shallot
1½ teaspoons hot bean sauce
1 teaspoon sugar
1½ tablespoons oil

Garnish

shredded cucumber

Preparation

Wash noodles in a strainer and leave aside. Mix cornstarch with chicken stock. Soak dried black mushrooms to soften. Chop all B ingredients coarsely.

Cooking

Combine B ingredients in a 2 liter (2 qt) shallow casserole. Microwave on power HIGH for 4 minutes, uncovered.

Add ingredients A. Microwave on power HIGH for 1½ minutes, uncovered.

Add the remaining ingredients. Cover and microwave on power HIGH for 8 minutes. Stir after 3 minutes of the cooking cycle.

Let the casserole STAND for 10 minutes, covered, before serving garnished with shredded cucumber.

Hum Yee Mai

Serves 4
Cooking time: 11½ mins
Standing time: 10 mins
Preparation: 15 mins
K cal: 295/serve

Ingredients
80 g (3 oz) saltfish
100 g (3½ oz) beansprouts
80 g (3 oz) chives

A

2 teaspoons chopped garlic
1½ teaspoons oil

200 g (7 oz) thin rice
    noodles

B

1⅓ cups chicken stock
½ tablespoon light soy
    sauce
1½ teaspoons dark soy
    sauce

Preparation

Slice saltfish thinly. Wash and pluck off 'tails' of beansprouts. Wash and cut chives into 3 cm (1 in) lengths.

Cooking

Sandwich saltfish slices between paper towels and microwave on power HIGH for 2 minutes. Chop coarsely.

Combine ingredients A in a 2 liter (2 qt) shallow casserole. Microwave on power HIGH for 3½ minutes, uncovered.

Add rice noodles and ingredients B. Cover and microwave on power HIGH for 6 minutes. Stir after 3 minutes of the cooking cycle.

Add beansprouts, chives and chopped saltfish and let casserole STAND covered for 10 minutes.

Stir evenly before serving.

Sea Kingdom

(photo page 152)

Serves 6
Cooking time: 9½ mins
Preparation: 15 mins
K cal: 190/serve

Ingredients
300 g (10 oz) rice noodle
    sheets (*hor fun*)
100 g (3½ oz) beansprouts

A

80 g (3 oz) fish fillet
100 g (3½ oz) shrimp
80 g (3 oz) cuttlefish
80 g (3 oz) crabmeat
1 tablespoon light soy sauce
1 teaspoon dark soy sauce
½ teaspoon sugar

B

2 teaspoons chopped garlic
1½ tablespoons oil

3 tablespoons chicken stock

Preparation

Lightly wash rice noodles sheets and cut into 1 cm (½ in) wide strips. Wash and pluck off 'tails' of beansprouts.

Cut fish fillet into thin slices. Shell and devein shrimp. Clean cuttlefish and cut into bite-sized pieces.

Cooking

Combine ingredients B in a 2 liter (2 qt) shallow casserole. Microwave on power HIGH for 4 minutes, uncovered.

Add ingredients A and microwave on power HIGH for 1 minute, uncovered.

Add rice noodle strips and chicken stock. Cover and microwave on power HIGH for 4½ minutes.

After 2½ minutes of the cooking cycle, add beansprouts, then cover the casserole and resume the cycle.

SAUCES & STOCKS

Sauces thicken evenly when microwaved, and require stirring only two or three times during the cycle. This is a definite advantage compared to conventional cooking where constant stirring is necessary to prevent burning.

Cover the cooking container with a paper towel or some waxed paper to prevent spattering.

Pineapple Chili Sauce

(photo page 160)

Cooking time: 24 mins
Preparation: 5 mins
K cal: 280

Ingredients
250 g (9 oz) pineapple
100 g (3½ oz) chiles
50 g (1¾ oz) garlic
1½ teaspoons salt

Preparation

Remove skin and 'eyes' of pineapple and chop finely.

Wash chiles, remove stems and blend till fine. Mince garlic to a paste.

Cooking

Combine all ingredients in a 24 cm (9 pt) casserole. Cover and microwave on power **HIGH** for 4 minutes. Then cover and simmer on power **LOW** for 20 minutes.

NOTE: *When cool, store in a sterilized jar and keep refrigerated.*

Preserved Bean Sauce

(photo page 160)

Cooking time. 6½ mins
Preparation: 5 mins
K cal: 445

Ingredients
A
100 g (3½ oz) preserved
    soy beans
30 g (1 oz) garlic
1½ tablespoons oil
1½ teaspoons sugar

B
1 teaspoon dark soy sauce
1 teaspoon cornstarch
1 cup water

Preparation

Blend preserved soy beans and garlic to a paste.

Cooking

Combine ingredients A in a 24 cm (9 in) casserole. Microwave on power **HIGH** for 3½ minutes, uncovered.

Add mixed ingredients B, cover and microwave on power **HIGH** for 3 minutes. Stir after every minute of the cooking cycle.

Sesame Oyster Sauce

(photo page 160)

Cooking time: 7 mins
Preparation: 5 mins
K cal: 220

Ingredients
1½ tablespoons sesame
    seed paste
½ cup oyster sauce
2 teaspoons ginger juice
2 teaspoons wine
1½ teaspoons sugar
1½ cups water
1 teaspoon cornstarch

Cooking

Combine all ingredients in a 24 cm (9 pt) casserole. Microwave on power **HIGH** for 2½ minutes, uncovered.

Next, simmer on power **MEDIUM** for 4½ minutes, still uncovered.

Sweet Chili Sauce

Cooking time: 4 mins
Preparation: 5 mins
K cal: 440

Ingredients
50 g (1½ oz) dried chiles
150 g (5 oz) tomatoes
2 tablespoons sugar
1 tablespoon oil
1 cup water
1 tablespoon light soy sauce

Preparation

Wash dried chiles and tomatoes and blend to a paste.

Cooking

Combine sugar and oil in a 20 cm (8 in) casserole. Microwave on power **HIGH** for 1½ minutes, uncovered.

Add all other ingredients and microwave on power **MEDIUM** for 2½ minutes, uncovered. Stir halfway through the cooking cycle.

Sauces (clockwise from left): Black hoisin, Sesame Oyster, Preserved Bean, Pineapple Chilli (pp. 158-9)

Chicken Stock

Cooking time: 1 hr 10 mins
Preparation: 5 mins

Ingredients
600 g (1 lb 5 oz) chicken
  bones left over from
  deboning chicken
1½ liters (3 pt) water
½ teaspoon wine

Cooking
Combine all ingredients in a 4 liter (4 qt) casserole. Cover and microwave on power HIGH for 10 minutes.

Next, simmer on power LOW for 1 hour, covered.

Allow stock to cool before straining through a cloth bag. Freeze in small quantities in plastic bags or paper cups and use as required.

Fish Stock

Cooking time: 40 mins
Preparation: 5 mins

Ingredients
600 g (1 lb 5 oz) fish bones
  and head
1 liter (1 qt) water
6 slices ginger
3 slices galangal

Cooking

Combine all ingredients in a 4 liter (4 qt) casserole. Cover and microwave on power HIGH for 10 minutes.

Next, simmer on power MEDIUM for 30 minutes, covered.

Cool stock before straining through a cloth bag. Freeze in plastic bags or paper cups until required.

Prawn Stock

Cooking time: 38 mins
Preparation: 10 mins

Ingredients
300 g (10 oz) prawn shells
  and heads
1 liter (1 qt) water
4 slices ginger
3 slices galangal

Preparation

Prawns must be washed before shells and heads are removed. Only shells and heads are used for stock.

Cooking

Combine all ingredients in a 3 liter (3 qt) casserole. Cover and microwave on power HIGH for 8 minutes. Next, simmer on power MEDIUM for 30 minutes.

Cool stock before straining through a cloth bag. Freeze in plastic bags or paper cups until required.

SNACKS & SWEETS

The selection of snacks offered here are substantial *dim sum* ('small eats') dishes that can if desired make up a meal. Many of these, such as Chung, Lor Bak Koh, Lor Mai Kai and Siew Mai, can be cooked many days in advance and frozen. Reheat on High for 1–2 minutes, depending on quantity, in a covered container.

Besides sweet desserts, several cooling herbal brews are described, their nutritional uses outlined in the recipes. Adjust the sweetness to your taste by adding more boiling hot water or sugar. Two ingredients must be mentioned in particular. Longan, which appears in many recipes, is believed to improve the spirit and sharpen intelligence, while our recipe for ground sesame seeds (Jee Mah Wu) is believed to darken grey hair!

Chung varieties (pp. 164, 166-7)

Cantonese Chung

(photo page 163)

Serves 6
Cooking time: 34 mins
Standing time: 15 mins
Preparation: 20 mins
K cal: 390/serve

Ingredients
16 bamboo leaves

A
2 teaspoons salt
2 teaspoons pepper
1½ teaspoons five-spice
    powder

200 g (7 oz) glutinous rice
100 g (3½ oz) dried green
    beans, skinless variety
150 g (5 oz) belly pork
50 g (1½ oz) dried shrimp
4 dried black mushrooms

B
3 tablespoons chopped
    garlic
2½ tablespoons oil

ball of thin twine or raffia
hot water to boil dumplings

Preparation

Wash and soak bamboo leaves overnight. Combine ingredients A and divide into 5 portions.

Wash glutinous rice in a strainer and soak in clean water overnight. Season with a portion of combined ingredients A.

Wash dried green beans and soak for 2 hours. Season with a portion of combined ingredients A.

Cut belly pork into 16 pieces and season with a portion of combined ingredients A.

Wash dried shrimp and season with a portion of combined ingredients A.

Soak dried black mushrooms, and when softened cut into 16 pieces. Season with a portion of combined ingredients A.

Cooking the Filling

Combine ingredients B in a small casserole and microwave on power HIGH for 4 minutes, uncovered.

Divide cooked ingredients B equally between the glutinous rice, dried green beans, belly pork, dried shrimp and black mushrooms.

Divide glutinous rice, dried green beans and dried shrimp into 16 portions.

Wrapping Dumplings

Assemble bamboo leaves, glutinous rice, green beans, belly pork, dried shrimp, and mushrooms.

Fold each bamboo leaf into a cone and fill with a portion of seasoned ingredients in the following order: ½ portion rice, dried green beans, belly pork, dried shrimp, mushrooms, and finally top with remaining ½ portion rice.

Fold the extended ends of the bamboo leaf to cover filling and secure with twine or raffia as shown in the diagram.

Repeat the process until all ingredients are finished.

Cooking the Dumplings

Put rice dumplings in a 5 liter (5 qt) casserole. Fill the casserole with hot water until ¾ full. Cover and microwave on power MEDIUM-HIGH for 30 minutes.

Let the casserole STAND for 15 minutes. Unwrap and serve.

Wrapping Chung

1 Fold bamboo leaf in half. Place your thumb (the left one if you are right-handed) about 1 cm (½ in) from one end – roughly where the arrow is, in proportion to the leaf width. Press with that thumb so the leaf comes up on either side.

2 Twist the top portion of the leaf into a cone. Fill the cone as instructed in the recipe.

3 Fold over the ends to cover rice, pressing down corners neatly.

4 Bring string twice around the parcel, pull tight and knot twice.

Tips

Practice Chung-wrapping using semi-cooked rice, which makes the package easier to hold.

You may use two short leaves, one partially overlapping the other to extend the length if both are too short to use alone. Overlapping leaves is also a way to avoid wasting leaves that have been punctured. Do not, however, use two leaves wholly overlapping each other or the parcel becomes bulky and untidy.

Spicy Chung should be full but Sweet Chung should not, as rice expands with alkaline water.

Try looping a bunch of string 1½ meters (5 feet) long over a long nail on a door, a pole or a strong hook. Knot to secure to nail, etc. It makes wrapping a lot easier if you know the other end of the string is secure.

Oil in the boiling water prevents rice from sticking to the leaves.

Baking soda is a suitable borax substitute but it results in a softer Chung.

Trim only after cooking, as a careless movement may puncture the leaves, resulting in the stuffing flowing out while cooking.

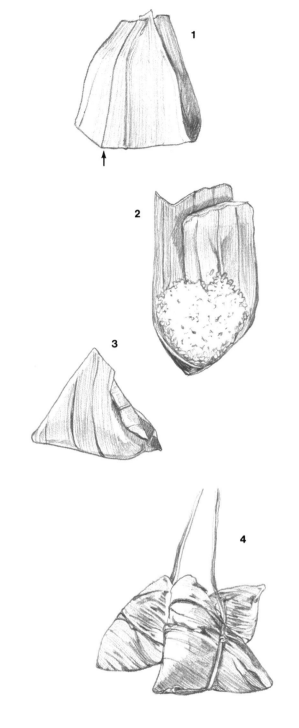

Savory Chung

(photo page 163)

Serves 6
Cooking time: 48½ mins
Standing time: 15 mins
Preparation: 25 mins
K cal: 550/serve

Ingredients

12–18 bamboo leaves
300 g (10 oz) glutinous rice
12 chestnuts
75 g (2½ oz) dried shrimp
200 g (7 oz) belly pork
5 dried black mushrooms
3 salted egg yolks

Seasoning

3 teaspoons dark soy sauce
1½ teaspoons five-spice
   powder
½ teaspoon sugar
2 teaspoons salt
½ teaspoon pepper

A

1 teaspoon chopped garlic
2 teaspoons chopped shallot
2 tablespoons oil

½ cup water

1½ teaspoons chopped
   garlic
2 tablespoons oil

ball of thin twine or raffia
hot water to boil dumplings

Preparation

The following must be seen to the previous day. Wash and soak bamboo leaves overnight. Wash glutinous rice in a strainer and soak in clean water overnight. Soak chestnuts overnight.

Wash and drain dried shrimp. Cut pork into 12 portions. Soak dried black mushrooms to soften, then cut in half. Quarter each salted egg yolk.

Combine seasoning ingredients and divide into 3 portions.

Cooking the Filling

Rice: Combine ingredients A in a 24 cm (9 in) casserole. Microwave on power **HIGH** for 4 minutes, uncovered. Add rice and ⅓ of the seasoning ingredients with ½ cup water and microwave on power **HIGH** for 4 minutes, uncovered. Set aside.

Dried Shrimp: Combine ½ teaspoon chopped garlic with 1 table-spoon oil in a 24 cm (9 in) casserole. Microwave on power **HIGH** for 2 minutes, uncovered. Add dried shrimp and ⅓ of the seasoning ingredients. Microwave on power **HIGH** for 2 minutes, uncovered. Divide into 12 portions. Set aside.

Pork-Chestnut-Mushroom Mix: Combine 1 teaspoon chopped garlic with 1 tablespoon oil in a 24 cm (9 in) casserole. Microwave on power **HIGH** for 3½ minutes, uncovered. Add pork, chestnuts, mushrooms and ⅓ of the seasoning ingredients. Cover and microwave on power **HIGH** for 3 minutes. Set aside.

Wrapping Dumplings

Assemble the following items: bamboo leaves, half-cooked rice, cooked shrimp, cooked pork-chestnut-mushroom mixture, salted egg yolk.

Fold each bamboo leaf into a cone and fill it with 2 teaspoons of half-cooked rice, 1 piece each of pork, chestnut and mushroom, a portion of dried shrimp, and a piece of salted egg yolk. Top with another 2 teaspoons half-cooked rice.

Fold the extended ends of the leaf to cover filling and secure with twine or raffia string as shown in the diagram for Cantonese Chung.

Repeat the process until all the rice is used up.

Cooking the Dumplings

Put rice dumplings in a 5 liter (5 qt) casserole. Fill casserole with hot water until ¾ full. Cover and microwave on power **MEDIUM–HIGH** for 30 minutes. Let casserole **STAND** for 15 minutes.

Unwrap and serve. Two of these dumplings make a very substantial meal.

NOTE: *Chung, a glutinous rice dumpling, makes its appearance in Chinese homes during the festival that occurs on the 5th day of the 5th Lunar Month. This festival commemorates the death of a Chinese poet who drowned himself rather than face dishonor. Fishermen would throw rice dumplings into the sea to feed his spirit. All Chung varieties keep up to 2 weeks. Steam before serving.*

Sweet Chung

(photo page 163)

Serves 6
Cooking time: 30 mins
Standing time: 15 mins
Preparation: 30 mins
K cal: 440/serve

Ingredients
20 bamboo leaves
300 g (10 oz) glutinous rice
½ tablespoon alkaline water
300 g (10 oz) red bean
   paste

ball of thin twine or raffia
hot water to boil dumplings
½ teaspoon borax

Preparation

Wash and soak bamboo leaves overnight. Wash glutinous rice in a strainer and soak in water with ½ tablespoon alkaline water for 4 hours.

Divide red bean paste into 20 portions.

Wrapping Dumplings

Fold each bamboo leaf into a cone and fill with first 1 tablespoon rice, next a portion of red bean paste, then top with 1 tablespoon rice.

Fold the extended ends of the bamboo leaf to cover filling and secure with twine or raffia as shown in the diagram for Cantonese Chung.

Repeat this process until all the rice is used up.

Cooking the Dumplings

Put rice dumplings in a 5 liter (5 qt) casserole and fill with hot water to cover the dumplings. Stir in borax.

Cover and microwave on power MEDIUM-HIGH for 30 minutes.

Let the casserole STAND for 15 minutes. Unwrap before serving.

NOTE: *This variety of dumpling can be kept for 2 weeks. Just steam for a short while before serving.*

Tau Sar (Red Bean Paste)

Cooking time: 1 hr 32 mins
Standing time: 15 mins
Preparation: 5 mins
K cal: 1560

Ingredients
150 g (5 oz) red beans
2¾ cups water

A
100 g (3½ oz) sugar
4½ tablespoons oil
⅔ cup water

Preparation

Wash red beans in a strainer and soak in clean water overnight.

Cooking

Combine red beans with 2¾ cups water in a 22 cm (9 in) casserole. Cover and microwave on power HIGH for 12 minutes. Next, microwave on power MEDIUM-LOW for 55 minutes.

Rub lightly and wash off the skin and drain skinless beans in a cloth bag.

Combine skinless beans with ingredients A in a 20 cm (8 in) casserole. Microwave on power MEDIUM-HIGH for 25 minutes, uncovered. Let casserole STAND for 15 minutes.

NOTE: *This recipe makes 300 g (10 oz) red bean paste (tau sar).*

Fah Sang Wu (Peanut Paste Dessert)

(photo page 170)

Serves 10
Cooking time: 19 mins
Preparation: 5 mins
K cal: 215/serve

Ingredients
250 g (9 oz) toasted peanuts
3 cups water
150 g (5 oz) brown sugar
1 cup milk

Preparation

Blend toasted peanuts with water and sugar to a fine paste in an electric blender or liquidizer.

Cooking

Place blended ingredients in a 4 liter (4 qt) casserole. Cover and microwave on power HIGH for 9 minutes. Stir halfway through the cooking cycle.

Stir in milk and microwave on power MEDIUM for 10 minutes, uncovered. Stir occasionally during the cooking cycle.

Serve hot.

Ginger Rice Drink

Cooking time: 10 mins
Preparation: 10 mins
K cal: 430

Ingredients
100 g (3½ oz) rice
150 g (5 oz) ginger

Preparation

Wash rice in a strainer. Scrape skin off ginger and chop finely.

Cooking

Place all ingredients on a dinner plate and microwave on power HIGH for 10 minutes, uncovered.

After 3 minutes of the cooking cycle, stir ingredients every minute to toast evenly.

Cool and store in an airtight container.

Ginger Rice Brew

Place 1 tablespoon of the toasted rice mixture in a cup and top with boiling water. Cover and leave the brew for 15 minutes before serving.

NOTE: *This drink is served to women after childbirth to remove 'wind' and keep them warm. Plain water, especially if cold, is usually not drunk during confinement.*

Gingko Nuts with Barley Drink

Serves 6
Cooking time: 40 mins
Standing time: 15 mins
Preparation: 15 mins
K cal: 160/serve

Ingredients
100 g (3½ oz) gingko nuts
    (*pak kor*)
50 g (1½ oz) barley

A
20 g (½ oz) dried beancurd
    sheet (*foo chook pei*)
150 g (5 oz) sugar

6 cups water

Preparation

Shell gingko nuts and peel off the skin. Halve and remove bitter embryo in the center.

Wash barley in a strainer. Break dried beancurd sheet into pieces and soak to soften.

Cooking

Combine gingko nuts with barley and 3 cups water in a 5 liter (5 qt) casserole. Cover and microwave on power HIGH for 10 minutes.

Add ingredients A and the remaining water. Cover and microwave on power MEDIUM–LOW for 30 minutes.

Let the drink STAND for 15 minutes before serving.

NOTE: *Pak Kor Yee Mai is the Cantonese name of this drink, which can be served hot or cold.*

Jee Mah Wu (Sesame Seed Dessert)

Serves 8
Cooking time: 13 mins
Standing time: 10 mins
Preparation: 10 mins
K cal: 190/serve

Ingredients
150 g (5 oz) toasted sesame
    seeds
½ tablespoon cornstarch
1½ tablespoons water
¾ cup sugar

A
2½ cups water
½ cup milk

Preparation

Blend toasted sesame seeds to a fine paste with some of the water for ingredients A in an electric blender. Mix together cornstarch and 1½ tablespoons water.

Cooking

Combine blended sesame seeds with sugar in a 4 liter (4 qt) casserole and microwave on power HIGH for 5 minutes, uncovered.

Stir in combined ingredients A and cover. Microwave on power MEDIUM for 8 minutes.

Immediately after the cooking cycle, stir in cornstarch mixture and let it STAND for 10 minutes before serving.

NOTE: *Appearances are deceptive! This thin black gruel makes a delicious dessert for those with a sweet tooth.*

From top: Lor Mai Kai (p. 173), Fah Sang Wu (p. 168), Woon Chye Koh (p. 177)

Loh Hon Kor (Buddha's Fruit Drink)

Serves 6
Cooking time: 25 mins
Preparation: 15 mins
K cal: 160/serve

Ingredients
A
**1 Buddha's fruit, 20 g (½
    oz)**
150 g (5 oz) longan meat
200 g (7 oz) winter melon
120 g (4 oz) brown sugar

4 cups water

Preparation

Wash and crush Buddha's fruit. Wash longan meat to rid it of dust and bits of shell and seed.

Scrape off hard skin of winter melon. Cut into small pieces, discarding seeds, and blend finely in an electric blender or liquidizer.

Cooking

Combine ingredients A in a 5 liter (5 qt) casserole. Cover and microwave on power HIGH for 10 minutes.

Add water and microwave on power HIGH for 15 minutes, uncovered.

NOTE: *This drink can be served hot or cold and is most refreshing on hot days.*

Loke Mei (Drink of Six Flavors)

Serves 10
Cooking time: 45 mins
Preparation: 5 mins
K cal: 100/serve

Ingredients
80 g (3 oz) longan meat
**80 g (3 oz) dried persim-
    mon**
**15 g (½ oz) dried magnolia
    petals (*pak hup*)**
**100 g (3½ oz) cooked lotus
    seeds**
20 g (¾ oz) *wai sun*
20 g (¾ oz) *yoke chok*
150 g (5 oz) rock sugar
10 cups hot water

Preparation

Wash longan meat to remove dust and bits of shell. Wash persimmon and slice thinly. Soak magnolia petals, then discard water.

Cooking

Combine all ingredients in a 5 liter (5 qt) casserole. Cover and microwave on power MEDIUM-LOW for 45 minutes.

NOTE: *This sweet drink can be served hot or cold as a dessert.*

Lor Bak Koh (Radish Pudding)

Serves 8
Cooking time: 20½ mins
Preparation: 20 mins
K cal: 180/serve

Ingredients

170 g (6 oz) rice flour
2½ cups warm water
50 g (1½ oz) dried shrimp

A

500 g (1 lb 1 oz) Chinese
**   radish**
¼ teaspoon five-spice
**   powder**
½ teaspoon pepper
½ teaspoon salt

B

1 teaspoon chopped garlic
2 teaspoons chopped shallot
4 tablespoons oil

Garnish

chopped spring onions and
**   Chinese parsley**

Preparation

Combine rice flour and warm water. Wash and chop dried shrimp.

Grate Chinese radish finely and squeeze out the juice. Combine the other A ingredients.

Cooking

Combine ingredients B in a 24 cm (9 in) casserole and microwave on power HIGH for 2½ minutes, uncovered.

Add chopped dried shrimp and microwave on power HIGH for 1½ minutes, uncovered. Add ingredients A, cover and microwave on power HIGH for 3 minutes.

Stir in rice flour mixture and microwave on power HIGH for 4½ minutes, uncovered. Stir after every minute of the cooking cycle to ensure even thickening.

Cover and microwave on power MEDIUM-LOW for 9 minutes.

Sprinkle with chopped spring onions and Chinese parsley and serve.

NOTE: *The pudding is usually cut to serving portions. It goes very well with pineapple chili sauce.*

Lor Mai Kai (Glutinous Rice Chicken)

(photo page 170)

Serves 4
Cooking time: 16½ mins
Preparation: 15 mins
K cal: 455/serve

Ingredients
200 g (7 oz) glutinous rice
8 dried black mushrooms
100 g (3½ oz) Chinese barbecued pork (*char siew*)
20 g (½ oz) Chinese sausages
150 g (5 oz) chicken pieces

Seasoning
½ teaspoon dark soy sauce
1 teaspoon light soy sauce
1 teaspoon wine
1½ tablespoons oyster sauce
¼ teaspoon sugar

A
1 teaspoon chopped garlic
3 tablespoons oil

²⁄₃ cup water
1 teaspoon oil

4 small bowls or pyrex cups

Preparation

Wash glutinous rice in a strainer and soak in clean water for 4 hours. Soak dried black mushrooms to soften.

Slice *char siew* and Chinese sausages to ½ cm (¼ in) thickness.

Marinate chicken pieces with half of the combined seasoning mixture.

Cooking

Combine ingredients A in a 24 cm (9 in) casserole. Microwave on power HIGH for 4 minutes, uncovered.

Add glutinous rice, remaining seasoning and ²⁄₃ cup water. Microwave on power HIGH for 6 minutes, uncovered. Set aside.

Put mushrooms with 1 teaspoon oil in a small casserole and microwave on power HIGH for 1½ minutes, uncovered. Set aside.

Divide seasoned chicken pieces and prepared ingredients into 4 portions.

Fill bowls or cups in the following order: seasoned chicken, mushrooms, *char siew*, Chinese sausage, and lastly the half-cooked rice.

Cover the cups with cling wrap and microwave on power HIGH for 5 minutes.

Turn cups over onto a serving plate. Remove cups and serve.

NOTE: *Lor Mai Kai is part of the dim sum ('small eats') range which can be eaten for breakfast or brunch.*

Lotus Root with Rock Sugar

(photo page 175)

Serves 6
Cooking time: 1 hr 6 mins
Preparation: 5 mins
K cal: 60/serve

Ingredients
150 g (5 oz) lotus root
6 red dates
80 g (3 oz) rock sugar
6 cups hot water

Preparation

Scrape skin off lotus root and slice to ½ cm (¼ in) thickness. Wash red dates and discard stone.

Cooking

Combine all ingredients in a 3 liter (3 qt) deep casserole. Cover and microwave on power HIGH for 6 minutes.

Next, simmer on power MEDIUM-LOW for 1 hour.

Siew Mai

(photo page 140)

Serves 10
Cooking time: 6 mins
Preparation: 20 mins
K cal: 170/serve

Ingredients
2 cooked saited egg yolks

A
100 g (3½ oz) shrimp
80 g (3 oz) water chestnuts
250 g (9 oz) belly pork

B
1 teaspoon salt
¼ teaspoon pepper
1 teaspoon wine
⅛ teaspoon baking soda

30 pieces *wonton* skin

Dip
sweet chili sauce

Preparation

Chop salted egg yolks coarsely.

Shell and devein shrimp. Remove skin from water chestnuts and chop all A ingredients together.

Season chopped ingredients A with ingredients B and divide into 30 portions.

Wrap each portion of prepared ingredients in 1 piece of *wonton* skin and top with some chopped salted egg yolk.

Place prepared Siew Mai in a large plate, spray them with water and cover the whole plate with cling wrap.

Cooking

Microwave Siew Mai on power MEDIUM for 6 minutes. After 3 minutes of the cooking cycle, spray with water and continue cooking.

Serve hot with sweet chili sauce.

NOTE: *Siew Mai is almost mandatory in dim sum ('small eats'), and is very popular as an hors d'oeuvre.*

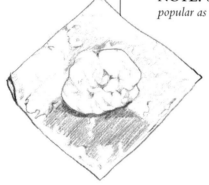

Sweet Bird's Nest

Serves 2
Cooking time: 40 mins
Preparation: 15 mins
K cal: 170/serve

Ingredients
15 g (½ oz) bird's nest
80 g (3 oz) rock sugar
1½ cups hot water

Preparation

Soak bird's nest. When soft, remove feathers.

Cooking

Combine all ingredients in an 18 cm (7 in) casserole. Cover and microwave on power LOW for 40 minutes.

NOTE: *Removing feathers from bird's nest is dreadfully tedious work. The higher the grade (and naturally the more expensive), the cleaner the ingredient.*

Winter Melon, Lotus Root – with Rock Sugar (pp. 173, 176)

Watercress, Candied Melon Soup

Serves 6
Cooking time: 1 hr
Preparation: 5 mins
K cal: 105/serve

Ingredients
300 g (10 oz) watercress
100 g (3½ oz) candied
**   melon**
100 g (3½ oz) sweet dates
6 cups hot water

Preparation

Wash watercress and cut into 3 cm (1 in) lengths.

Cooking

Combine all ingredients in a 5 liter (5 qt) casserole. Cover and microwave on power MEDIUM-LOW for 1 hour.

Winter Melon with Rock Sugar

(photo page 175)

Serves 4
Cooking time: 1 hr
Preparation: 15 mins
K cal: 180/serve

Ingredients
1 winter melon, 2 kg (4 lb
**   6 oz)**
50 g (1½ oz) red dates
120 g (4 oz) rock sugar
3 cups hot water

Preparation

Wash winter melon and cut a section 2 cm(1 in) from the top for a cover. Scoop out the seeds and pulp, leaving a 1½ cm (½ in) thick shell.

Wash red dates and discard stone.

Fill the winter melon with rock sugar, red dates and hot water. Replace the cover and secure with toothpicks.

Cooking

Place prepared melon in a 5 liter (5 qt) casserole. Cover with cling wrap and microwave on power LOW for 1 hour.

NOTE: *This sweet drink is believed to soothe the throat and improve the complexion.*

Woon Chye Koh (Savory Rice Pudding)

(photo page 170)

Serves 6
Cooking time: 12 mins
Standing time: 10 mins
Preparation: 10 mins
K cal: 230/serve

Ingredients

A
120 g (4 oz) rice flour
50 g (1½ oz) glutinous rice
    flour
2 cups hot water

B
150 g (5 oz) preserved
    Chinese radish
50 g (1½ oz) dried shrimp
50 g (1½ oz) shallots
30 g (1 oz) garlic
3 tablespoons oil

C
2 tablespoons light soy
    sauce
½ teaspoon sugar
⅓ tablespoon water

Preparation

Combine ingredients A, stirring well. Divide mixture into 8 portions and place each portion in a small Chinese soup bowl. Cover with cling wrap.

Chop ingredients B coarsely.

Cooking

Microwave rice mixture on power MEDIUM for 6 minutes. Let it STAND for 10 minutes.

Combine ingredients B in an 18 cm (7 in) casserole. Microwave on power HIGH for 4½ minutes, uncovered.

Add ingredients C and microwave on power HIGH for 1½ minutes, uncovered.

To serve, remove rice cakes from bowls and top with a teaspoonful of cooked ingredients.

Yam Cake

(photo page 140)

Serves 8
Cooking time: 16 mins
Standing time: 10 mins
Preparation: 15 mins
K cal: 250/serve

Ingredients

A
170 g (6 oz) rice flour
30 g (1 oz) cornstarch
3 cups water
1 teaspoon salt

B
450 g (1 lb) yam
30 g (1 oz) dried shrimp
100 g (3½ oz) belly pork
30 g (1 oz) Chinese sausages
½ teaspoon five-spice
    powder

C
1 teaspoon chopped garlic
1 teaspoon chopped shallot
2 tablespoons oil

Preparation

Combine ingredients A, stirring well. Peel and dice yam. Wash dried shrimp and chop coarsely. Dice belly pork and Chinese sausages.

Cooking

Combine ingredients C in a 2 liter (2 qt) shallow casserole. Microwave on power HIGH for 3½ minutes, uncovered. Add ingredients B and microwave on power HIGH for 2½ minutes, uncovered.

Add combined ingredients A and microwave on power HIGH for 3 minutes, uncovered. Stir mixture every minute of the cooking cycle until it thickens. Cover and microwave on power LOW for 7 minutes.

Let casserole STAND for 10 minutes, covered, before serving.

MENU PLANNER

Chinese New Year Reunion Dinner for 10
Stuffed Freshwater Prawns (p. 57)
Good Things Come Your Way! (p. 41)
Jade and Ivory (p. 133)
Wang Choy Chow Sow (p. 69)

Chinese New Year reunion dinner is celebrated on the eve of the Lunar New Year. All family members gather in the house of the head of the family for this special meal. The names of all the dishes must have auspicious meanings and the ingredients used sound like auspicious words. After the meal, the family members stay on till midnight to welcome the new year. At about 11 p.m. the traditional would change into new clothes and pray to the Heaven God or Tin Sun. Once the prayers start, the floor must not be swept for this would cause all the luck to be swept away.

Shopping list

red dates
dried black mushrooms
dried scallops (25 g/1 oz)
12 dried oysters
black moss seaweed (20 g/$\frac{2}{3}$ oz)
water chestnuts (40 g/1$\frac{1}{2}$ oz)
1 carrot
green peas

1 pig's spleen
2 roasted pig's forelegs
fillet of Spanish mackerel (300 g/10$\frac{1}{2}$ oz)
crabmeat (150 g/5$\frac{1}{4}$ oz)
10 large freshwater prawns (800 g/1 lb 12$\frac{1}{4}$ oz)

broccoli (200 g/7 oz)
cauliflower (200 g/7 oz)
3 Taiwanese cabbages
Chinese parsley

Avoid buying all ingredients on the morning of Chinese New Year Eve as not only will everything that sounds remotely auspicious be horrifically expensive, but some of them may not be available by then. Shopping should be done two weeks ahead and ingredients frozen where necessary, and fresh greens bought a few days before the event.

MENU PLANNER

1 Remove all ingredients from the freezer and defrost in the microwave oven.
2 While defrosting other ingredients, prepare sauces and set aside.
3 Cook Wang Choy Chow Sow immediately after defrosting.

Noon

Organize all the ingredients required, recipe by recipe.

Ready for dinner

Informality is the keynote of this dinner which is a gathering, after all, of people intimately known to each other. Cook course by course, setting the oven for the next course before bringing out one.

1 While inviting family members to take their place, cook the first course which means 'Bring Out Joy and Laughter'.
2 When the Stuffed Freshwater Prawns are out of the oven, cook the second course, 'Good Things Come Your Way'.
3 Drink a toast after the second course, then cook the vegetable (Jade and Ivory) as it has to be eaten hot. When the Jade and Ivory is out of the oven, warm up the last dish on power High for 5 minutes.
4 Serve Wang Choy Chow Sow with fresh lettuce – *sang choy* is Chinese for rare luck, and Wang Choy Chow Sow 'Luck be at your hand'.

MENU PLANNER

Birthday Dinner for 10
Cheong Meng Foo Kwai (p. 129)
Lotus Pond (p. 134)
Wheel of Fortune (p. 94)
Birthday Noodles (p. 154)

Longevity, every year will come, wheel of fortune - these are some of the names of the recipes chosen. Celebrating birthdays is not an annual affair. The Chinese believe that birthdays should be celebrated only when one has reached fifty and is blessed with grandchildren. Thus, birthday celebrations begin at fifty, and to mark the end of each decade thereafter, sixty, seventy, etc. Widows and widowers, however, celebrate on odd-numbered years: fifty-one, sixty-one. . .

In the morning, preferably between 8 and 9 a.m. (8 is *fatt*, prosperity and 9 is *kau*, long life), after prayers, the children and grandchildren offer tea to the birthday person, in order of seniority. They receive *hong bao* (red packets of money) in exchange. The accepted greeting from friends and relatives is 'Long life and many more to come' and appropriate gifts are cloth and money in even numbers, in red packets. Taboos are unrelieved black or white cloth and gifts of shoes, clocks or watches.

Shopping list

dried sweet beancurd sheets (*tim chook*, 10 g/⅓ oz)
wonton noodles (200 g/7 oz)
deep-fried fish cakes (100 g/3½ oz)
18 dried black mushrooms
10 straw mushrooms
20 quail's eggs
red dates

1 plump roasting chicken (over a kilo, about 3 lb)
lean pork (350 g/12¼ oz)
shrimp (300 g/10½ oz, shelled)

1 small pumpkin (just over a kilo, about 2½ lb)
beansprouts (80 g/3 oz)
Tientsin cabbage (80 g/3 oz)
2-3 carrots
lotus root (350 g/12¼ oz)
Chinese parsley

Shop for ingredients on the day of celebration

MENU PLANNER

1 Immediately after marketing, prepare chicken and pumpkin recipes, then refrigerate till ready to cook.
2 Cut all ingredients.

Two hours before dinner

1 Cook the chicken and let it stand. If it is cold by dinnertime, warm up on power High for 3-4 minutes.
2 Next, cook the stuffed pumpkin.
3 Once the guests have arrived, start cooking the lotus root and noodles.

Dinnertime

Set the table with individual plates, bowls, spoons and chopsticks. Serve all dishes at once, with serving spoons and chopsticks.

MENU PLANNER

Buffet Party for 20
Golden Fish Rolls (p. 38, x 3)
Stuffed Chicken Wings (p. 92, x 3)
Salad Cup (p. 135, x 2)
Cold Chicken Towers (p. 86, x 2)
Loh Hon Kor (p. 171, x 3)
Char Cheong Meen (p. 156, x 3)

Planning a buffet party is simple but to prepare and cook it single-handed is tedious. The microwave oven will save you much trouble and you can entertain as often as you like.

Shopping list

several dried black mushrooms
dried cuttlefish strips (40 g/1½ oz)
firm white beancurd squares (*tau foo*, 150 g/5¼ oz)
thick yellow noodles (600 g/1 lb 5 oz)
Szechuan vegetable (150 g/5¼ oz)
longan meat (450 g/1 lb)
3 Buddha's fruit (60 g/2¼ oz)
brown sugar (360 g/12¾ oz)
cornflakes

lean pork (300 g/10½ oz)
belly pork (200 g/7 oz)
36 large chicken wings (about 3 kilos/6¾ lb)
chicken breast meat (400 g/15 oz)
fish fillet (900 g/2 lb)
shrimps (300 g/10½ oz)

green peas (200 g/7 oz)
winter melon (600 g/1 lb 5 oz)
3-4 heads lettuce
carrots (500 g/1 lb 2 oz)
yam bean (550 g/1 lb 3 oz)
Chinese parsley
1 cucumber
30 French beans
9 asparagus shoots

Shop for ingredients on the eve of the party.

MENU PLANNER

After marketing

Upon your return from the supermarket:
1 Debone chicken wings, season them and refrigerate till the next day.
2 Slice and season the pork.
3 Brew Loh Hon Kor. Cool and chill, ready to serve the next day.
4 Prepare and cook Chicken Towers, chill for serving.
5 Cut ingredients for the remaining recipes and refrigerate.

Afternoon of the party

1 Cook filling for Salad Cups.
2 Cook gravy for Char Cheong Meen, and set casserole aside to warm up before serving.
3 Prepare Stuffed Chicken Wings and Golden Fish Rolls to be ready for cooking.

Ninety minutes before the party

1 Start cooking.
2 Set the table.
3 Warm food only as the first guests arrive. Only button-pushing is required by this stage.

MENU PLANNER

Quickie Dinners

Black Bean Spare Ribs (p.64)
Steamed Beancurd with Dried Shrimps (p. 115)
Spicy Sauce Steamed Fish (p. 42)
Spicy Asparagus (p. 141)

Thinking of what to cook on a busy day can be a problem. With a microwave oven and a freezer you will be saved much harassment. Let us look at the recipes in our list. At least one time-consuming step can be accomplished days or weeks ahead, on a spare weekend, to be whipped out when you really need the extra breather or when an unexpected guest stays on for dinner.

Black Bean Spare Ribs

This can be prepared after marketing and frozen. When ready to serve, defrost for 8 minutes then continue cooking as described in the recipe.

Steamed Tau Foo with Dried Shrimps

A large quantity of dried shrimps can be fried as described in the recipe when time permits. Store in an airtight jar. The other steps of the recipe take next to no time.

Spicy Sauce Steamed Fish

Spicy sauce can be prepared in bulk and stored in the refrigerator, to be ladled out every time it is required. There is no need to prepare a fresh lot each time you stem fish - or prawns, or spare ribs for that matter.

Spicy Asparagus

Many individual portions of ingredients A can be prepared and frozen in plastic bags. When required, defrost for 2½ minutes then proceed with the cooking. Asparagus can be cut into required lengths after marketing and stored in the crisper, when required, soak in water for 15 minutes.